The Wild Horses *of* Chincoteague National Wildlife Refuge

THE HOOFPRINTS GUIDE TO

The Wild Horses
of Chincoteague
National
Wildlife Refuge

Written and Illustrated by
Bonnie U. Gruenberg

QUAGGA
PRESS

The Hoofprints Guide to the Wild Horses of Chincoteague

Copyright © 2015 by Bonnie U. Gruenberg.

ISBN 13: 978-1-941700-05-1

Library of Congress Control Number: 2015936706

Published by Quagga Press, an imprint of Synclitic Media, LLC
1646 White Oak Road • Strasburg, PA 17579 • www.quaggapress.com

Also by the author
  The Wild Horse Dilemma: Conflicts and Controversies of the Atlantic Coast Herds (Quagga Press, 2015)
  The Hoofprints Guide Series (Quagga Press, 2015)
    Assateague
    Chincoteague
    Corolla
    Ocracoke
    Shackleford Banks
    Cumberland Island
  Essentials of Prehospital Maternity Care (Prentice Hall, 2005)
  Birth Emergency Skills Training: Manual for Out-of-hospital Providers (Birth Guru/Birth Muse, 2008)
  Hoofprints in the Sand Wild Horses of the Atlantic Coast (as Bonnie S. Urquhart; Eclipse Press, 2002)
  The Midwife's Journal (Birth Guru/Birth Muse, 2009)
  Hoofprints in the Sand: Wild Horses of the Atlantic Coast, Kindle Edition (Quagga Press, 2014)
  Wild Horses of the Atlantic Coast: An Intimate Portrait, Kindle Edition (Quagga Press, 2014)

Forthcoming
  Wild Horse Vacations: Where To See the East Coast Herds and What Else To Do While You're Visiting (Quagga Press, 2015)
  Wild Horses! A Kids' Guide to the East Coast Herds (Quagga Press, 2015)
  Birth Emergency Skills Training, 2nd Edition (Synclitic Press, 2015).

Introduction

The wait was worth it. I had beached my kayak on a sand bar and stood in the pleasantly moist muck for hours waiting for the Chincoteague ponies of the south herd to begin their annual swim-back to Assateague. One year, the fire department granted me a press pass that allowed me to photograph the pony swim to Chincoteague at optimally close range. For the swim-back, this intimate access is available to anyone willing to paddle to the site and wait in the hot sun. And then, there they were. In a matter of minutes, a diverse assortment of mares, stallions and young foals had swum the channel and were surging across the sandbar right in front of me. The small crowd of paddlers gaped in astonishment and delight as the ponies hurried by, eager to return to their home range. Then the majority mounted their boats and followed the retreating phalanx of ponies, a shifting mosaic of primary colors against the rippling blue of the bay.

When I first started researching the wild horses in the mid-1990s, I was surprised to find that wild horses lived on a number of Atlantic barrier islands and had once ranged along much of the Atlantic coast. They made their first hoofprints there not long after the arrival of early European settlers, and in time they ran free on innumerable North American islands and peninsulas from the Caribbean to Canada. I learned that small herds remained on the coast of Virginia, North Carolina, Maryland, and Georgia; on Sable Island, off Nova Scotia, Canada; and on Great Abaco Island in the Bahamas. Each population of horses has its own character, its own history, and its own set of problems. In most cases, these animals have made a unique contribution to local history, and each herd has its own detractors and defenders.

After my first book, *Hoofprints in the Sand: Wild Horses of the Atlantic Coast*, was published in 2002 by Eclipse Press, I dove in deeper, interviewing experts, evaluating the evidence, and monitoring the herds. I explored management conflicts that encompassed political, economic, and cultural issues as well as purely scientific ones. I studied storms and shipwrecks, equine behavior and genetics, history, epidemiology, barrier-island dynamics, sea-level rise, beach development, and the perpetual clash of viewpoints. I studied hundreds of documents, from historical papers to scholarly journals to court transcripts, so that I might accurately present the pertinent issues. Distilling all this information, I tried to present all sides of the issues fairly so that readers might reach their own conclusions. The result is *The Wild Horse Dilemma: Conflicts and Controversies of the Atlantic Coast Herds* (Quagga Press, 2015) the most comprehensive work ever published about these horses.

Wild Horse Dilemma is exhaustively researched, copiously documented, and peer-reviewed; but at 600 pages it may be too long for many people eager to learn about a particular herd. For readers with limited time, I created the Hoofprints Series. Excerpted from *Wild Horse Dilemma* and containing additional photographs, each Hoofprints book presents a single Atlantic Coast herd in sufficient detail to satisfy both the layman and the academic.

I take all my wild-horse photographs though telephoto lenses that let me to keep my distance. When horses approached, I retreated. My goal has been to remain so peripheral to their lives, they will forget that I am nearby. Because countless people have stroked them, fed them, and lured them, some can be momentarily docile, occasionally indifferent, or routinely bold and pushy in the presence of people. As anyone bitten or trampled can attest, they are no less wild than horses that avoid human contact. When we impose ourselves and our desires on their lives, when we habituate them to our presence, when we teach them to approach us for food and attention, we rob them of their wildness. When we treat them as we would their domestic counterparts, we miss the opportunity to observe them in a natural state, that is, to appreciate the things that make them irresistibly attractive. We miss the very point of driving past thousands of their tame kin to seek them out. We create something like a petting zoo hazardous to us and to them. If we truly love and respect wild creatures, we must learn to stand back and enjoy watching them from afar. Only then can they—and we—know the real meaning of wildness.

As the earth's dominant species, we have the power to preserve or destroy the wildlife of the world and the ecosystems in which they live. The choices we make regarding wild horses are far-reaching. We alter their destiny whether we act or choose to do nothing. We can begin to deal wisely with wild horses by understanding the facts and discovering how the threads of their existence are woven into the tapestry of life. Only through understanding can we hope to make rational, educated decisions about the welfare of these fascinating, inspiring animals.

Bonnie U. Gruenberg
Strasburg, Pennsylvania
March 1, 2015

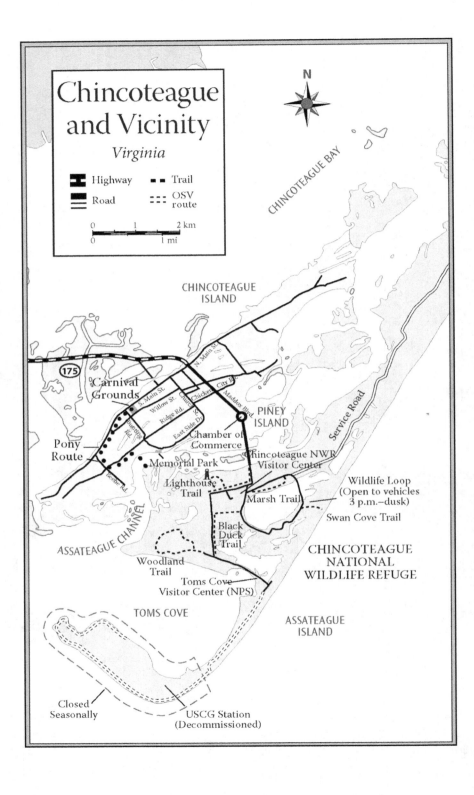

The spectacle was mesmerizing. At the urging of the cowboys, a multitude of wild horses charged into the stillness of Assateague Channel and swam, heads dotting the slate-blue surface, lips curled and nostrils narrowed. Mares nickered encouragement to wild-eyed colts as they plunged into water made turbulent by hundreds of flailing hooves. Saltwater Cowboys shouted and cracked bullwhips for emphasis, but the ponies did not need much urging.

Swimming comes naturally to them. In the wilds of Assateague, they often ford tidal creeks and seek refuge from insects by immersing themselves in the waters of the bay. Sometimes ponies make the swim to Chincoteague of their own accord, singly or in groups, forcing the cowboys to conduct an impromptu roundup to restore them to their Assateague range.

As their hooves found purchase in the sticky marsh mud, they emerged onto Chincoteague. A prancing, snorting throng of sleek, dripping horses rose out of the bay—palominos, chestnuts, buckskins, and pintos—like mythical beasts rising from enchanted waters in a fairy tale. It was enough to make a photographer put down her camera and gawk in slack-jawed astonishment.

Chincoteague, a small island community on the Eastern Shore of Virginia, historically made its living from the sea. Chincoteague's delectably salty oysters put the town on the map, but town was thrust forever into the limelight in 1947, when Marguerite Henry's book *Misty of Chincoteague* brought the tradition of Pony Penning to the attention of children all over the world. Today the promise of seeing wild ponies (and eating tasty seafood) brings thousands of annual visitors to this unique little island.

Although there are festivals and activities in Chincoteague all year long, the most famous attraction is the herd of free-roaming ponies that lives across the channel on Assateague Island in the Chincoteague National Wildlife Refuge. Traditionally, on the last Wednesday and Thursday of July, locals round up the ponies on their Assateague home ground, swim them across the channel to Chincoteague, and

Every July, almost 200 wild ponies enter the waters of Assateague Channel for the annual swim. Heads and backs above the water, the ponies move to shore in a cohesive mass.

sell spring foals at auction. Every year Pony Penning draws crowds in the tens of thousands and attracts international media coverage.

The periodic penning of Assateague Ponies has gone on for hundreds of years, and the Chincoteague Volunteer Fire Company has maintained the tradition since 1924. The fire company has held the Firemen's Carnival, Pony Penning, and sale annually, except for a lapse in 1943 and 1944 due to World War II. The proceeds of the auction go toward maintaining the herd and covering operating expenses for the fire company, the legal owner of the ponies on the Virginia end of Assateague. "The men and women of the fire company work long, long hours to do what we do," says Denise Bowden, executive secretary and spokesperson for the firefighters (personal communication, February 5, 2011).

Pony Penning is the culmination of the month-long Firemen's Carnival. Each year, approximately 30–40 Saltwater Cowboys participate in the roundup, swim, and parade. About half are members of the fire company; the rest take their horses on an annual trek to the island to participate. The Cowboys typically work their way up through the ranks, helping with menial tasks at first, and only sliding into the coveted cowboy role if a rider dies or retires. "If a Cowboy or fireman has

Hoofprints Guide

As their hooves find the bottom, they rise from the water like mythical sea creatures.

a son or male relative who wants to get involved, they will take him on," says Pam Emge, co-author of *Chincoteague Ponies: Untold Tails*. "The Fire Company says that women can become Saltwater Cowboys, but you never see a woman rider. They are all men, every one" (personal communication, September 7, 2014).

On the weekend before the drive, the Cowboys take their own horses to Assateague and gather the wild ponies that live on the Chincoteague NWR. They confine the 50-odd adult horses and their foals from the southern end of the refuge in a corral on Beach Road. To the north, a second pen near Swan Cove holds the larger part of the herd, about 100 adult ponies and their foals. The ponies are intelligent and have indelible memories—they know the drill.

The joining of the two groups, an event known as the Beach Walk, takes place on the last Monday in July. Crowds start to form before daybreak as spectators claim prime spots along the beach. The Fish and Wildlife Service scouts the beach for piping plover nests before the pony drive, and sometimes requires the cowboys to use an alternative route to avoid disturbing broods. It seems there is always a light mist rolling off the ocean as the restless crowd waits, sometimes for hours. Then, emerging like a mirage from the shimmering morning mist, the herd materializes. About 150 ponies, flanked by slicker-clad Saltwater Cowboys, move slowly down the shoreline through the lap of breaking waves. Occasionally a cowboy must reclaim an excited nervous foal which darts across the beach or into the surf. Making a

At the auction grounds, mares and foals are herded into the barn (above) and through a sorting chute that directs foals into stalls (facing page) and mares back to the corrals.(below). Mares hear their youngsters calling, and whinny their plaintive replies (below).

Chincoteague

sharp right-hand turn toward the crowd, the ponies surge by the spectators and down Beach Road to join the southern herd at the corrals.

Within the corrals, excited horses collect into groups, break into a run, scatter, and collect again. Foals whinny frantically for their dams. Stallions suddenly thrown together battle to establish dominance and reassemble their scattered mares. Equine family groups cluster around hay piles, squealing and arguing with others as they jockey for the best feeding spots. Occasionally, a pregnant mare gives birth. All the while, people cluster along the fence, fascinated by equine dramas witnessed at close range. Prospective pony owners eye the foals critically, choosing favorites for Thursday's bidding.

The fire company extends a hose from a fire truck and fills the troughs with cool water. All day Monday and Tuesday, people flock to the pony pens to watch the milling animals with insatiable interest. A veterinarian evaluates the health of each animal and looks for illness and injuries. Heavily pregnant mares, old or weak ponies, and newborn foals are exempt from the swim and are taken to the carnival grounds by trailer.

People flock from all over the world to witness the Pony Swim. Countless others watch the event live on television programs such as *Good Morning America*. On the last Wednesday of July, Saltwater Cowboys herd the ponies from the pens to the edge of the channel that separates Assateague from Chincoteague. There they await slack tide, the interval between high and low tides when the current in the channel is at its weakest. Well in advance of the event, boats form a corridor through which the ponies will swim. The wait for slack tide seems interminable.

The crowd suddenly snaps to attention as the Coast Guard fires a red starburst rocket to signal the start of the main event. As thousands watch, cowboys herd the horses into the channel. Initially they hesitate, and then a seasoned pony who has been though previous swims splashes into the water and heads for the distant shore, followed by another and another. The crossing takes only about 7–10 min, whereupon the ponies emerge from the channel waters onto Chincoteague soil.

Suddenly there are ponies rising from the water *en masse*, dripping brackish water and looking very pleased with themselves. The first foal to reach Chincoteague is dubbed King or Queen Neptune and

At the joining of the herds, the world-famous Saltwater Cowboys drive the north herd down the beach to the corrals on Beach Road, where the south herd awaits. Spectators lined up along the beach get an up-close view of lively ponies against the backdrop of sunrise over the ocean.

is traditionally raffled off that night—in 2009, the fire company sold more than 6,000 tickets at a dollar each. The seasoned adults and bewildered youngsters move onto a small meadow of lush green grass to rest and recover.

Then the cowboys press them into motion again. The large, lively herd of ponies parades up Main Street to another set of holding pens at the carnival grounds, where they will stay until Friday morning. Moving shoulder to shoulder, the animals snort and prance past wide-eyed spectators at the curbside. Occasionally, the cowboys must guide a rogue pony back to the herd after it breaks away from the group and runs across a lawn or driveway.

Thursday is auction day. The best seats are staked out well in advance, but any persistent bidder can get close enough to the action to participate. It is usually very hot, with abundant flies and mosquitoes and frequently a passing shower. Anyone may bid, and it is possible to place a bid unintentionally by waving to a friend or swatting a fly.

Beginning early in the morning, staff members separate foals from their mothers and begin the process of presenting each youngster to the admiring crowd for bidding. Volunteers lock hands around previously unhandled foals, grabbing the tail and under the belly, and attempt to guide them around the arena while the weanlings leap, pitch, and try to escape. Some foals recognize the futility of rearing and kicking, so they sit or lie down and refuse to move.

By midday, nearly every foal will have a new owner. The veterinarian is available to draw a Coggins, test, vaccinations, deworming, and issue a health certificate before the foal leaves the island. Most are loaded into trailers by 5:00 p.m. Friday and trundled to faraway new homes. Foals younger than one month old are usually allowed to remain with their mothers after the sale, to be claimed in the fall by their buyers. Some youngsters are sold as "turn-backs" or "buy-backs" and are returned to the herd.

Children venture to the island hoping to place a winning bid, but not everybody gets a pony. Because about 1,000 bidders compete for about 60–70 foals, most would-be pony owners return home disappointed. And Chincoteague foals sell for prices that would challenge the wallet of the most hardworking child.

Horses tend to bring out the best in people, and it may be true that the folklore and legends surrounding the Chincoteague Ponies make that equine magic all just a little more special. In 2004, the Feather Fund was founded to help children of limited means purchase a Chincoteague Pony.

The story is poignant. In the summer of 1995, Carollynn Suplee, feeling grateful to have survived her recent brain surgery, attended the auction with the hope of buying a turn-back pony. By the time she arrived, the turn-backs had all been sold. Deeply spiritual and feeling the need to give something back after surviving her illness, she donated money that allowed two horse-loving sisters to bid on and win Sea Feather, a pony that they otherwise could not afford.

She returned to the island annually, prayed for direction, and each year helped a child purchase a foal. She became known as the "Pony Fairy" until her death in 2003. The following year the Feather Fund was established as a nonprofit in her memory. Children age 10 to 14 may apply for a pony and demonstrate that they have saved a portion of the money on their own, have experience with ponies, and are able to maintain a foal. The Feather Fund committee chooses a winner from letters, photographs, and videos, and then helps the child select and bid for a foal. Sometimes two or three foals are awarded to lucky children.

After the auction, unsuccessful bidders may acquire ponies though alternative means. Foals born after Pony Penning and into the fall are sold during the October roundup, and several breeders on Chincoteague Island offer foals and trained horses for sale each year. The Chincoteague Pony Rescue is a nonprofit organization in Ridgely, Maryland, that rehabilitates abandoned, neglected, abandoned and abused Chincoteague Ponies and places them in loving homes.

Desirable coat color inflates the prices more than anything else—chestnuts typically fetch lower prices than pintos with flashy markings. One can usually determine whether a foal will be buckskin, palomino, or chestnut by the color of the juvenile coat, but there is always the possibility that a foal will mature with a different color than expected. Foals usually go through several coat-color changes before arriving at their adult coloration, and even then many horses change color seasonally. R. Owen Hooks estimates that over the last 50–60 years, about 40% of the Chincoteague herd has been pinto; 30% chestnut; 20% bay; 8% buckskin, dun, or grulla; and 2% other colors such as palomino, gray, cream, roan, or black. Rare colors usually fetch higher prices, except dun, which tends to sell for less than average.

Prior to the 1920s, the horses were solid-colored. E.L. Vallandigham (1893, p. 28) wrote, "The ponies are from 11 to 14 hands high, and weigh from 650 to 750 pounds. There are many bays, sorrels and blacks, a few grays and occasionally a roan."

In 1910, the Phoenix *Arizona Republican* described the herd thus:
> The ponies are very irregular in size, for they are often found as tall as the bronco and the mustang of the west, and again as small as the Shetland pony. They are as a rule weedy and inclined to be leggy, with rought [*sic*], uneven, sunburned coats. Light bays and sorrels predominate. A fair number of brown bays will be found, while black, white and [d]un colored ponies are exceedingly rare. ("The Wild Ponies of a Virginia Island," 1910, p. 9)

Marguerite Henry's best-selling *Misty of Chincoteague* remains very popular and is responsible for a good amount of the tourist traffic to Chincoteague each year. In 1961 the story became the successful movie *Misty*.

Misty was a real pony, born on the Beebe ranch—not on Assateague, as in the book. Henry fell in love with the week-old Misty while visiting Chincoteague and bought her from Clarence Beebe for $150. Paul and Maureen Beebe, who became characters by the same names in the book, halter-broke and gentled the pony during her stay on the Beebe ranch. When Misty was weaned, Henry had her shipped out to her home in Illinois to provide inspiration while she wrote her famous story. Although *Misty of Chincoteague* is not strictly factual, the setting is true to life and gives a fairly accurate portrayal of Pony Penning in the 1940s. Misty died in 1972 at the age of 26.

More than 60 years after the publication of Misty of Chincoteague, the story is as popular as ever. Visitors can see Misty and her daughter Stormy at the Museum of Chincoteague Island—stuffed! There is a bronze statue of Misty as a foal prominently displayed on Main Street, and Misty's hoofprints still grace the concrete walk in front of the Island Roxy Theater, where her movie premiered. The Beebe ranch still stands.

Each year charitable individuals purchase several foals and donate them to the fire company for re-release on Assateague as breeding stock. This custom began after the Ash Wednesday storm in March 1962, which drowned many ponies. A 1964 article in the Norfolk *Virginian-Pilot* mentioned "Yankee" stock added to the "storm-wasted" Assateague herd so that the pony penning could continue (Grey, 2014).

Pregnant Misty weathered the storm safely in the Beebes' kitchen and soon after delivered her third and final foal, aptly named Stormy, at a veterinary clinic in Pocomoke City., Md. In 1963 Stormy became the heroine of her own book: *Stormy, Misty's Foal.* This book was also a fictionalized account—three of the protagonists (Grandpa Clarence, Grandma Idy, and Paul) were dead by then.

The Ash Wednesday storm devastated the wild herd. Twentieth Century Fox made the movie *Misty* available for special showing along the East Coast with the proceeds used to purchase ponies previously sold at auction to replenish the herd. This tradition was eventually formalized into the buy-back program in the 1990s.

When the foals are taken from their mothers on auction day, they are initially frantic to reunite, and they whinny incessantly to one another. After witnessing the affection evident between the mare and

Marguerite Henry's book *Misty of Chincoteague* has been loved by children since its publication in 1947. A bronze statue of Misty stands prominently on Main Street.

Although many of the events in the Misty books are fictitious, Misty was a real pony, and her hoofprints remain in the sidewalk in front of the Island Roxy theater. Misty and her foal Stormy can be seen at the Museum of Chincoteague Island—stuffed!

Chincoteague

her offspring, some people are upset by the forced separation. They say it is heartless to take a foal from its mother at such a young age. Indeed, in the wild, horses often nurse for a year, or even two. Domestic horses are typically weaned between 4 and 6 months of age.

Additionally, at the time of the auction, these mares are often already pregnant with next year's foal. Mares who nurse one foal while gestating the next have higher rates of spontaneous abortion. Weaning the foals in July increases the likelihood that they will deliver healthy foals the following spring. On the other hand, mares burdened with nearly continuous pregnancy and lactation tend to have shorter lives and poorer health than mares who have few pregnancies.

Although early weaning is associated with increased mortality in foals living wild on barrier islands, it appears to have no adverse effect on the health of foals bought at auction. Research on orphaned foals, most of them weaned at birth, has shown that early weaning presents no long term disadvantage if the foals are properly fed and socialized. In the first weeks of early weaning, foals grow more slowly than their suckling counterparts, but quickly recover lost ground. There is no difference in size or behavior between foals weaned early, including those weaned at birth, and those allowed to suckle their dams for 4–6 months. In fact, many of the mainland-raised ponies grow far taller than their counterparts remaining on the island. Like a puppy who cries her first night away from her mother, the foals call and search at first, but quickly settle into the new routine. The youngest foals stay with their mothers until the October roundup.

On Friday, most of the remaining horses are trailered back to the North portion of the refuge, and the Cowboys herd the rest to the water's edge for a short swim to swim to the south end. Generally, by the time the herd steps out of the water on Assateague, the mares have stopped looking for their foals, although there are anecdotal accounts of mares swimming back to Chincoteague in an attempt to retrieve them.

In 1971, the Humane Society of the United States and the American Horse Protection Association protested the Chincoteague Pony Penning, claiming that it was blatantly abusive to the animals. In its November 1971 newsletter (quoted in Spies, 1977, p. 20), the organization said, "Three HSUS investigators observed the annual roundup and auction of the wild ponies at Chincoteague, Va., last summer and

A mare named 15 Friends of Freckles shepherds her youngster out of harm's way as two stallions, Wild Bill (left) and the mare's sire, the half-Arabian North Star (right) move into battle.

concluded it was the cruelest activity they had ever witnessed." The agency claimed that newborn, sick, and dehydrated horses were being forced to make the swim. It alleged that day-old foals were being taken from their mothers and loaded into the backs of station wagons for long drives to distant states. Often their feet were tied to minimize struggle. Buyers purchased nursing foals without realizing that they would need to bottle-feed them every two hours around the clock. People ignorant of proper horse care and not equipped to maintain livestock would get caught up in the excitement and rashly buy a foal because it was cute. It is not easy to raise a foal from undisciplined babyhood to become a reliable mount, even in the best of circumstances, and these unprepared non-equestrians were clearly out of their depth, much to the foals' detriment.

Ronald Rood's 1967 book *Hundred Acre Welcome* (p. 76) offers some corroboration of these claims. "Ruefully we had to admit that not a few of those ponies, bought so hastily and with so many good intentions, would probably end up as mere curiosities, pets—sort of summer romances that hung around through the winter. Worse still, if they went to homes smaller than our farm, they might become definite liabilities, finally to be sold, or given away to any taker." Rood allowed his son to impulsively bid on a young foal. After the transaction was completed, Rood wondered, "But now what do we do? How in the dickens do I get a pony out of here and back to Vermont?" (1967,

Dripping wet and looking self-satisfied, the ponies emerge from the water to graze on the lush marsh grass. In 2011 Kimball's Rainbow Delight (right), a daughter of North Star, was first to emerge, followed closely by Island Breeze.

p. 79). Since Rood had a commitment in Raleigh, N.C., after their stay in Chincoteague, they could not send the colt back to Vermont; so a local friend recommended taking the colt with him. "In your station wagon. It will be a cinch!" (Rood, 1967, p. 80). Rood writes, "Others besides ourselves were adopting makeshift means with regard to their ponies." He described a man who put a brown-and-white filly in the back of his pickup truck. She "slipped in her struggle to keep her balance as he drove away" (1967, p. 80). Another woman removed the back seat of her car, shoved it onto the trunk, and loaded her foal into its place. "I wondered how they would make out on their trip back to New Jersey" (1967, p. 81). Rood transported his pony crated in a Volkswagen Microbus, unloading him at rest stops, tidying his stall, and dumping the dirty bedding in trash cans.

Feeding the pony was another matter. After the foal was purchased, a firefighter told Rood, "This one's smaller than most of 'em. . . . So I doubt if he's weaned from his mother very much. You might have to feed him with a bottle for a couple of weeks" (1967, p. 86). The foal rejected the bottle, but eventually accepted soaked grain. The colt

A young foal resists the efforts of a volunteer fireman to load him into the motor home that stands ready to take him to his new home. July 30, 1970. Photograph courtesy of the *Baltimore Sun*.

found a new home on Rood's farm in Vermont as a family pet and a tourist attraction.

In the 1970s, the fire company enlarged the corrals by 30 ft/9 m. Old, sick, newborn, and pregnant mares at term were exempted from the swim. It discontinued hot branding and later implemented nondestructive freeze-branding. It sold very young foals only to those willing to take on the responsibility of bottle-feeding and supplied samples of milk replacer. The fire company also ensured that new owners transported their foals in approved conveyances. A 1973 follow-up report (in Spies, 1977, p. 20) stated, "HSUS attended the annual wild pony swim and auction in Chincoteague, Va., in July and concluded that the event has improved to the point of being completely humane."

Yet in 1992 and 1995, The Humane Society of the United States again protested the event. This time they disapproved of the "wild pony rides," traditionally held on Thursday after the auction. Unbroken wild ponies, many of them lactating mares that had just lost foals to the auction, were ridden bareback rodeo-style, bucking, wheeling, and frantic beneath courageous contestants. This practice was halted in 1996.

The fire company says that the accounts of cruelty were exaggerated or false and assert that they always try to act in the best interest of the ponies. Humane organizations made a fuss over the use of bullwhips in rounding up the horses; but on closer investigation, they found that the cowboys used whips as noisemakers, not to strike the ponies.

Sometimes natural disaster befalls the penned ponies. The fire company reports that in 2012, a lightning strike in the corral tragically killed the pregnant 2008 mare Dream Dancer, unique for her curly black-and-white coat. Similarly, in 1981 the fire company reported two mares and a colt dead from a lightning strike in the Assateague corral.

At every Pony Penning, the fire company, which legally owns all the ponies, inspects the new crop of foals and determines whether any exceptional colts and fillies should be returned to the herd as breeding stock. In the past, unsold foals were also returned to Assateague—but in recent years, every foal has sold easily. Each year, the fire company generously donates the purchase price of a buy-back foal to a charity, such as Ronald McDonald House or the Hospice of the Eastern Shore.

On the day of the auction, Chincoteague Volunteer Fire Company staff parades the foals in front of the crowd and sells them to the highest bidders. Most youngsters resist handling, rearing and leaping in an effort to break free or simply lying on the ground and refusing to budge. This colt's dished face, broad forehead, large eyes, and small muzzle speak of Arabian lineage.

As tax-deductible contributions to the fire company, buy-backs typically fetch much higher prices than the ponies sold to leave the island, and bidding is fierce. The winning bidder chooses a name for the pony, poses for a photograph, and then signs the pony over to the fire company. For the life of the buy-back ponies and their descendants, purchasers feel a personal connection to Assateague and enjoy knowing that "their" horses remain wild on the island.

The "Buy-Back Babes," a group of women from all over the United States—Florida, Illinois, Pennsylvania, California—have collectively purchased a number of ponies for re-release on the island. "We got

Touched for the first time by human hands, young foals often buck, rear, and attempt to bolt when paraded in front of bidders. Some simply lie down and refuse to move.

Chincoteague 31

15 Friends of Freckles, a loudly-marked pinto mare, listens to her foal calling to her from the auction pen. Chincoteague Ponies tend to have good conformation and excel in disciplines from hunter-jumper to endurance and Western pleasure.

our name, the Buy-Back Babes, because our husbands will not let us buy one and bring it home, thus we have to buy the buy-backs!" says Jean Bonde, who has been a Buy-Back Babe since the group came together in 2002 (personal communication, July 23, 2010). Anyone can become a Buy-Back Babe by approaching a member of the group at the pony auction and contributing money toward the purchase of a turn-back foal. "Whoever donates money to buy a pony is a Buy-Back Babe," says Bonde (personal communication, July 23, 2010). "There are approximately 36 Buy-Back Babes and about 32 others interested in ponies who want to receive e-mails talking about pony happenings." Some Buy-Back Babes purchase other turn-back foals independently of the group. They also assist the Feather Fund to help children buy ponies. Once, when a woman from Connecticut bought a foal but could not afford to ship it home, the Buy-Back Babes purchased the foal from her, a chestnut named Gideon, and donated it to the Feather Fund to be given to a child.

Between Pony Pennings, the Buy-Back Babes make frequent visits to the Chincoteague NWR to observe the horses. They take photographs and share them via e-mail, discussing Mystery's new pinto foal to Spirit and how 4-year-old Prince was beginning to challenge the harem stallions for dominance. They know each animal intimately by name or nickname, habits, preferred ranges, and sometimes lineage. "We are like little girls, we get so excited when we do see ones we recognize," says Bonde (personal communication, July 23, 2010).

In 2007, the Buy-Back Babes paid a record $17,500 for Tornado's Prince of Tides, a palomino-and-white colt colored much like the legendary Misty. He was doubly prized because few stallions are returned to Assateague. "Usually the cowboys pick out the ones they want to keep, but in several instances we had picked out a few before the auction, went to the cowboys and said we wanted to bid on one particular one," says Bonde (personal communication, July 23, 2010). "These are the ones that cost us the most money because we said we would take the bids all the way to the top."

Prince reigned as the record-setting pony for 7 years. Then in 2014, Catherine Miller of Peru, Illinois, bid $21,000 for a black and white buy-back filly out of Leah's Bayside Angel by the stallion Sockett To Me. That year, the average price per pony was $2,772, and the fire company earned $149,700 from the pony sale.

The winter of 2009–2010 was brutal, with powerful storms and significant flooding. Four buy-back foals went missing and were presumed dead, but no bodies were found. The other three buy-backs from that year were in good health. One of the foals lost was a very special filly named Suzy Q. She was named for Buy-Back Babe Suzanne Craig, who succumbed to pancreatic cancer in 2009. Another of the missing foals was the offspring of E.T., a buy-back purchased solo by Bonde in 2002.

At the Maryland end, horses also died during the winter of 2009–2010, but these were all elderly. "We lost 6 horses during the winter," says Allison Turner, biological science technician at Assateague Island National Seashore (personal communication, February 17, 2011). "Three were 30 years old, and the others were in their mid-20s. It was normal seasonal mortality."

Saddened over the loss of the foals, the pony committee agreed to give the Babes a filly to replace Suzy Q. The women selected Gidget's

Beach Baby, a pinto filly out of Gidget, their 2002 buy-back mare. To reduce future losses, the pony committee agreed to shelter weanling buy-back foals at the carnival grounds for their first winter, a trade-off between "wildness" and an increased chance for survival. The pony committee monitors them and ensures they have plenty of hay, grass, and water, and visitors can peer at them through the chain-link fence.

Monitoring the wild ponies is labor intensive for the fire company. Denise Bowden explains, "The Chincoteague Volunteer Fire Company's number one priority is to save lives and protect property—after that it's all about the ponies and nothing else" (personal communication, February 5, 2011).

The brawny sorrel stallion Surfer Dude apparently believes that he and his mares should have the run of the entire refuge. His band regularly escapes from their fenced rangeland at the end of Woodland Trail. They swim out into the bay and around the fence to graze on what they must see as the greener grass. "Beautiful Surfer Dude. I think more people know him than any other horse," says Bonde (personal communication, July 23, 2010). "He has two lead mares to guide him along, so they basically go where they want to go and he goes along with it." Every time they make a foray into forbidden territory, the refuge staff calls the fire company. Volunteers leave their day jobs to round up the escapees and replace them in their enclosure. In 2010, they escaped so persistently that the fire company confined them in the Beach Road corral for the duration.

Managing a wild horse herd presents numerous challenges not typically faced by volunteer fire departments. "We regard these beautiful animals as a gift from God," says Denise Bowden. "As much as they are wild animals—and believe me they are wild—they are also gentle creatures that sometimes need a little extra care when the elements get rough" (personal communication, February 5, 2011).

Each April, as spring starts to take hold, the ponies are gathered and a veterinarian assesses the health of each pony, administers vaccinations for Eastern and Western encephalitis, tetanus, West Nile virus, and rabies, draws blood for necessary tests such as Coggins, and checks mares for pregnancy. At the July roundup, the veterinarian performs another health check, and separates the ponies too young, old or debilitated to participate in the swim. He estimates the age of the foals before they enter the auction ring, and signs health

A mare with hypocalcemia rolls in pain while her hungry young foal urges her to rise. Intravenous infusion of calcium resolved the problem for this mare. The foal was weaned to a bottle and sold at auction to a buyer willing to become his surrogate mother by feeding him every 2 hours around the clock.

certificates for the foals that have been sold. In October, the ponies are gathered for a health assessment before winter and to be wormed with Eqvalan®, a drench dewormer. Foals that were too young for weaning in July or that were born after Pony Penning are removed from the herd and sold. In 2014, Dr. Charles Cameron, DVM, of the Eastern Shore Animal Hospital was recognized for serving the wild pony herd for 25 years.

Even though the fire company is the legal owner of all horses on the refuge, people who have purchased buy-back foals sometimes become heavily invested in their welfare and complain to the pony committee if they show any signs of compromised health. The fire company walks a very thin line, committed to increasing the health and survival of the ponies while keeping them as wild as possible. "The Chincoteague Volunteer Fire Company is doing the best we can with what we have," said Roe Terry, former public relations officer for the fire company (personal communication, July 27, 2010).

The public generally prefers that the ponies live wild and free with no interference, but also prefers that they always have adequate food, water, and health care. These two states are often mutually exclusive.

A female yellow-rumped warbler waits helplessly in a mist net for an ornithologist to free her. Before she is allowed to fly away, she will be weighed, measured, and banded. Thousands of migrating songbirds pass through the refuge each fall, and biologists collect important data on them.

Over the centuries, the fittest—and sometimes the luckiest—ponies have survived on Assateague to contribute their genes to the next generation. On the Maryland end of Assateague, the ponies are managed as wild animals and live with minimal interference by humans. Disease is seen by the National Park Service as a normal occurrence for wild horses. The horses at the north end of the island may be weakened by a harsh winter or a dry summer, or they may stand strong until conditions improve.

Every organization charged with the responsibility of managing wild horses needs to decide how much human intervention is appropriate. Management options run the gamut from keeping hands off, as with the wild horses of Nevada, to providing food, shelter, reproduction assistance, and health care, as with the herd on Ocracoke, N.C.

Though their ancestors ran free on the island for hundreds of years, Ocracoke Banker horses have been stabled in barns, corrals, and pastures since 1959. Not one individual alive today has experienced any more freedom than the average stabled horse. In fact, when Hurricane Isabel flattened the Ocracoke pony pen in September 2003, the horses stood out in the sand-covered road and waited patiently for people to come with hay and grain. Park Service ranger Laura Michaels jokes, "They were looking at their pony watches, saying 'It's been a day, where's my food?'" (personal communication, May 22, 2010).

Western ranches such as the famed Montana Horses allowed their several hundred horses to run free in the hills from autumn to mid-spring with minimal human intrusion. The horses lived as wild until the April roundup, when they were gathered and herded 30 mi/48 km to the ranch. From there, they were leased to work at guest ranches, camps, and trail-riding stables for the summer. These ranch horses experienced a much greater degree of freedom most days of the year than the Ocracoke horses have at any point in their lives.

At the "total dependence" end of the continuum, horses cannot be considered wild. Because humans are entirely responsible for the welfare of the Ocracoke horses, they are halter-broken for safe handling and maintained at a healthy weight, with proper hoof and veterinary care. Breedings are planned for optimal genetic diversity while preserving historical Banker bloodlines. When Hurricane Isabel blew down the barn, a stronger, safer one was built. They are fed hay and grain and watered in troughs, and they enjoy grooming, scratching, and pats from their handlers. At the price of freedom, they live longer, are better nourished, and are healthier overall than their free-roaming ancestors. Rather than survival of the fittest, this herd persists through survival of the favored.

At the other end of the continuum, the Cumberland Island, Georgia, herd roams free without any interference from people. These horses live as they wish from birth to death, choose their own mates, live with parasites, find their own water sources, eat whatever the island provides, and generally run the course of any illnesses without intervention from people. They may have more health issues and often have shorter lifespans than domesticated horses. Valuable genes may be lost because a particular horse never finds a mate. But they are free.

Autonomy versus greater safety and health is a trade-off for people, too. Helmet laws, smoking restrictions, emissions testing, mandated seat belts and infant car seats set limits on our behavior, for good or ill. People want safer environments and good health, but chafe when laws restrict personal freedoms.

"The Buy Back Babes, fire department and the refuge struggle with where the line should be drawn," said Lou Hinds, former Chincoteague NWR manager (personal communication, May 21, 2010). "If they are truly a wild population of ponies living their lives on a barrier beach island, they should be living at the mercy of Mother Nature. If they are dependent on people taking care of all their needs, they become just another managed herd of horses."

Horses cannot tell us whether they prefer an indulged existence in domestication or unfettered autonomy with a more precarious health status. The entities that decide the fate of the horses must place each herd somewhere on the wildness continuum, and no matter what they decide there will be compromises and trade-offs. Every intervention intended to improve the health and wellbeing of the horses takes them farther from the wild end of the gamut. Keeping horses wild means minimal intervention, but failure to provide adequate food or water is usually seen as neglect and cruelty. There are no indisputably correct answers and few easy decisions.

The Chincoteague firefighters are volunteers who balance their responsibilities to the community and to the horses with day jobs and families. They maintain the fences on the refuge and run the carnival and the events of Pony Penning week. When there is a fire, medical emergency, or a problem with the ponies—for example, when Surfer Dude's band escapes from the south enclosure—they respond with alacrity. Many, like Roe Terry, have belonged to the organization for much of their lives.

Assateague Island is fortunate to have escaped the clutches of civilization, although man has left his mark in many places. Archaeological sites on and around the island include the remains of eight shipwrecks, two of them Spanish, U.S. Lifesaving Service stations built beginning in the 1870s, a presidential yacht that sank in 1891, several abandoned villages, and 19th-century fish and salt factories.

On the Chincoteague NWR, the buildings of the U.S. Fish and Wildlife Service and the Park Service cluster along Beach Road, leaving most of the refuge undeveloped and for the most part inaccessible to the public. At least five federally listed threatened or endangered species breed on Assateague, and protected marine animals regularly

Wearing thick winter coats, these foals spent their first winter well fed and protected from the elements at the Chincoteague fairground. Though this confinement temporarily removed them from freedom, it increased the likelihood of their survival.

visit Assateague's offshore waters. A number of paths and roads, including a scenic loop around an artificial pond, give the visitor an overview of the refuge's features and habitats.

The Chincoteague NWR allows up to 150 adult ponies to live on its property in two barbed wire enclosures through a special-use agreement with the Chincoteague Volunteer Fire Company, which owns and manages the herd. The actual number of ponies is often below this maximum threshold: on August 31, 2012, there were 134 ponies on the refuge; 22 stallions and 112 mares. Each November, the fire company pays the refuge $1,500 for an annual grazing permit. Although the ponies are allowed on the refuge, they are not necessarily welcome. Hinds commented, "I've been told that the Fish and Wildlife Service has made it very clear to the firemen that we prefer not to have the ponies on the refuge" (personal communication, May 21, 2010).

According to Keiper & Houpt (1984), approximately 74% of the Virginia mares foaled in any given year, typically April through June, and about 80% of the foals were removed at Pony Penning. In contrast, the foaling rate for the Maryland herd was 57% in the days before immunocontraception.

While conducting a study of compensatory reproduction in feral horses in October 1989, Turner and Kirkpatrick collected urine or fecal samples from 40 Maryland mares (10 of which were lactating) and 48 Chincoteague mares (2 of which were lactating). The team tested urine for creatinine, estrone conjugates, and progesterone metabolites and tested feces for total estrogen and progesterone metabolites. These methods have proven 100% accurate in detecting pregnancy in domestic horses. The team found no difference in abortion rate between the two herds, even though the pregnancy rate was nearly twice as high in the Chincoteague herd, and concluded that "the differential foaling rates between the 2 herds is determined by October pregnancy rates, and not by fetal loss after approximately 90–150 days postconception" (Kirkpatrick & Turner, 1991, p. 650).

The paper went on to say that other researchers had shown the critical period for pregnancy loss in domestic mares to be days 25–31, and that the 1989 research showed a fetal loss rate at 90 days similar to that reported in domestic mares after day 45 postconception. They attributed the differential in foaling rates to lactational anestrus, the suppression of ovulation in lactating mares, and speculated that when foals are weaned early, the mare is likely to come into heat and become pregnant soon after.

Equine gestation averages 340 days, usually ranging from 327 to 357 days, but pregnancies as long as 399 days have been documented. This variation seems to have evolved to improve the survival of each foal by synchronizing reproduction with the seasons. Mares typically come into heat a week or so after foaling. If no pregnancy results, she will return to estrus at about 30 days postpartum, and every 3 weeks thereafter until the end of the breeding season. A mare that conceives during her foal heat will typically maintain a foaling interval of about one year. Pregnancy rates are 10–20% lower when a mare is mated during her foal heat.

Chincoteague foals are typically born in April, May, and June each year. If weaning at Pony Penning brought mares into estrus, then the following year's foals would be conceived in August and born in predominantly in July. A mare bred on August 15th would deliver a foal between July 12 and July 27 the following year. "Mares come into post-partum estrus 7–10 days after foaling, and in many cases they are successfully bred during that post-partum estrus, so some mares only have one estrus each year," says Dr. Ronald Keiper, a zoologist

Chincoteague Ponies receive veterinary inspections in April, July, and October and are treated for illness and injury when necessary. The veterinarian places a sticker on the back of each horse upon vaccination. The buckskin mare escorting her foal is Poco Latte, the smallest adult pony in the herd.

who has studied free-roaming barrier island horses for 40 years (personal communication, May 19, 2011). Keiper explains,

> Nursing a foal does not prevent that post-partum estrus. Mares become pregnant quickly and then for the next 11 months, they must "feed" their developing fetuses and provide milk for lactation. That strains the health of the mare, so if she is stressed by disease or a cold, wet winter with poor-quality winter food, she may abort the developing fetus. She has invested less in that fetus than she has in the foal, so she sacrifices the fetus (personal communication, May 19, 2011).

Lucas, Raeside, and Betteridge (1991) examined estrogen levels in the feces of 154 unmanaged free-roaming mares on Sable Island, Nova Scotia, over 4 years and found that fetal loss after day 120 was 26.0% overall (yearly variation 9.6–37.3%), and yearlings abort about 70% of conceptions. Of mares greater than 2 years of age that did not foal in the spring, about half had aborted foals after 120 days' gestation. Kirkpatrick and Turner noted a comparable rate of late pregnancy loss in both the Maryland and Virginia herds and concluded that mares of both herds pregnant in October have a fetal loss rate similar to that reported for domestic mares after 45 days of conception. Lactation imposes great energy demands on the mare, particularly in the first 12 weeks. A domestic mare produces an average of 3 gallons/11.4 L of milk a day during the first 5 months of lactation, the equivalent of 3% of her body weight. On the Maryland end of Assateague in the late 1980s, lactating mares often lost weight, had low body condition scores by the end of the summer, and appeared "unable to ingest enough food for the demands of peak lactation" (Rudman & Keiper, 1991, p. 456). Malnutrition is a known cause of abortion in mares. It appears that nutritionally challenged lactating mares are more likely to miscarry foals before October.

In other words, weaning a foal during Pony Penning does not make a mare more likely to get pregnant. But if she is already pregnant from an early postpartum estrus, weaning in July makes her more likely to carry her current pregnancy to term and deliver a healthy foal the following spring. Veterinary care and supplemental feeding of the Chincoteague NWR herd may also decrease the rate of pregnancy loss.

Two decades of managed reproduction have changed the Maryland herd so that researchers are unlikely to duplicate Kirkpatrick and Turner's findings from the late 1980s. Whereas Virginia mares continue to foal predictably in mid–late spring, out-of-season births rose to 26% among their Maryland kin by 2001, under the influence of immunocontraceptives.

The majority of Chincoteague Ponies are maintained on a parcel within the refuge that runs from north of the wildlife loop to the Virginia-Maryland line. About 805 acres are occupied by the freshwater impoundments of South Wash Flats, Old Fields, Ragged Point, and a portion of North Wash Flats. During the summer, the ponies graze on 2,695 acres/1,091 ha of lush forage. During severe storms, gates are opened to give the ponies access to the White Hills, a maritime forest growing atop an old ridge of dune, the highest ground in the refuge. An additional 704 acres/285 ha of the north range is managed during the summer as piping plover habitat to mitigate for the nesting habitat used as a parking area for the public recreational beach. In late fall the north refuge ponies use this parcel as winter habitat.

The 547-acre/221-ha section at the south end of the island supports another group of adult horses and their foals. This parcel

Egrets rest on the backs of ponies in the marshland of the south pasture. This lowland has grown progressively wetter over the years.

includes Black Duck Creek and all of Black Duck Marsh and comprises 70% marsh and grasslands and 30% maritime forest. A number of natural freshwater pools usually provide drinking water, but in drought conditions, they use troughs filled by the fire company or drink brackish water.

Historically, about 100 horses were maintained on the north range and 50 on the south. Rising sea level, however, has rendered the south parcel increasingly boggy, and in August 2012, 21 horses lived on the south compartment, with 113 on the north.

Horses are not the only potential threat to piping plovers (*Charadrius melodus*), seabeach amaranth, (*Amaranthus pumilus*) and other endangered species. On Assateague, over-sand vehicles such as pickup trucks are allowed to drive on 16 mi/26 km of open beach (12 mi/19 km in Maryland, 4 mi/6 km in Virginia). Beach driving is a popular activity, and as many as 145 vehicles are allowed access to the Maryland over-sand route at any one time. This heavy traffic disrupts the beach surface, leads to increased sand movement, impedes the formation of new dunes, and endangers shorebird habitat.

Whereas the Park Service works to help Assateague return to a more nearly natural state, the Fish and Wildlife Service actively manages its natural areas to make them more hospitable to desired wildlife species. Fourteen artificial freshwater ponds cover more than 2,623 acres/1,061 ha of the refuge. These impoundments create freshwater wetlands for waterfowl in winter and wading birds in summer as well as reptiles, amphibians, and other wildlife. Water is deeper in the spring and dries up over the summer, concentrating the populations of fish and eels; so when wading birds have young in the nest, food is easier to obtain. Alternately, the impoundments can be drained to provide nesting habitat for the endangered piping plover.

The ponds were dug 20–30 years ago to provide habitat for waterfowl. At that time the ocean was farther away, and the dunes were higher. Now only a series of small dunes separates the ponds from the ocean, and with Hurricane Sandy in 2012, water ripped through the beach, flooded the ponds, tore apart the pavement on Beach Road, and opened Avocet Inlet from Swan Cove to the sea. When the inlet spontaneously closed a short time later, only a narrow ribbon of beach divided the pond and the ocean.

The Chincoteague NWR tries to conserve and protect wildlife, giving priority to threatened and endangered species, and it is a breeding ground and sanctuary for songbirds and migratory waterfowl. The diversity of habitats on the refuge—beach, dunes, salt marshes, freshwater wetlands, maritime forests, estuaries, and ocean—appeals to a wide range of wildlife.

These habitats make Assateague a desirable stopover for birds migrating along the Atlantic Flyway. Spring and fall see a procession of species from songbirds to raptors and abundant waterfowl, some resident species and some passing through. The National Audubon Society designated the Virginia end of Assateague a Global Important Bird Area. The seashore is a primary feeding area for shorebirds, and the birds in turn are food for migrating peregrine falcons.

Four species of sea turtle swim the offshore waters, and loggerhead (*Caretta caretta*) and green sea turtles (*Chelonia mydas*) occasionally nest on the sandy beaches. The ocean off Assateague is also home to six species of baleen whales, five of which are endangered; 16 species of toothed whales and dolphins; four species of seals: and occasionally the endangered West Indian manatee (*Trichechus manatus*).

After the annual July Pony Penning, the south-end horses swim back to Assateague and regroup on their home ranges.

Right whales winter off Assateague and are occasionally spotted from the beach. The Atlantic northern right whale (*Eubalaena glacialis*) is highly endangered, with an estimated North Atlantic population of only 200.

The endangered Delmarva fox squirrel (*Sciurus niger cinereus*) was introduced to Chincoteague NWR in an attempt to increase its population. Once common from New Jersey and Pennsylvania to the Delmarva Peninsula, by the 1920s it was extinct in all states except Maryland. Between 1968 and 1971, 30 of these squirrels were released on the refuge to form a successful breeding colony.

Species considered detrimental to the mission of the Fish and Wildlife Service are controlled or eliminated, including native raccoons and introduced red foxes and mute swans. The three key unwanted species that compete at the table with the island's wanted wildlife are exotic sika deer, non-migratory nuisance Canada geese, and reintroduced Chincoteague Ponies. The refuge keeps these species under tight control—the ponies through annual removal, the deer through hunts, and the geese through egg addling.

To "addle" an egg is to remove it from the nest, kill the embryo without changing the appearance or texture of the egg, then return it to the nest so that the mother will continue to incubate it. If the mother believes the egg will not hatch, she will begin laying again. A common method endorsed by the Humane Society of the United States is to suffocate the embryo by painting the shell with mineral oil.

Shrub thickets provide nesting habitat for songbirds and a wind-break for wildlife. The White Hills stabilize the island and provide habitat and high ground for raccoons, ponies, deer, and other animals.

Where Assateague Island is widest, high ground develops and habitats diversify maximally. Where the island is narrow, most notably at the north end, overwash and salt spray reduce diversity of plant communities, but provide optimal habitat for seabeach amaranth and piping plovers. Assateague widens from north to south, and therefore the Chincoteague NWR supports a greater variety of habitats.

According to Hinds (personal communication, May 21, 2010), there is good reason to believe that Assateague will not be one long island over the next 100 years, but an archipelago, divided by a series of new inlets. This is a reasonable prediction because geological processes have torn Assateague asunder, then made it whole again several times just since European contact. Hinds said,

> It would not be responsible or sustainable for the federal government to attempt to prevent the division of the island, or to repair it if it should happen . . . we at the refuge are following the lead of the Park Service; we are just letting Mother Nature to do her thing. We are not building dunes or replacing dunes. We are allowing the island to migrate to wherever it wants to go.

The nor'easter of November 2009, which included the remains of Hurricane Ida, was a lesson in the futility of trying to restrain the forces of nature. Locals say that Assateague had not seen a storm of that magnitude since the early 1990s. It washed away the parking lot at Toms Cove, removed artificial dunes, and kicked up about 40 tons/36 metric tons of debris onto the shore.

Every time a storm wreaks chaos with the parking area, the Park Service restores it. Between 2002 and 2012 the parking lot was replaced four times, each episode draining between $200,000 and $700,000 of taxpayer money. Even small storms cause considerable damage, while significant hurricanes such as Irene in August 2011 narrow the beach and render the parking area unusable.

The 2009 nor'easter defiantly disarticulated an artificial reef built in the 1970s and spat nearly 2,000 tires onto the beach to become a cleanup headache for the Park Service and the refuge. When offshore sediment deposition and loss of shell bottom decreased the diversity

This map, drawn in 1651 by John Farrer and updated by his daughter Virginia, depicts Chincoteague ("Cingoto Ile") but not Assateague, places the Pacific Ocean just to the west of the Appalachians, and suggests a Northwest Passage through the Hudson River. Courtesy of the Library of Congress, Geography and Map Division.

and abundance of fish, in the 1950s private organizations developed tire reefs to provide habitat for marine life. The state of Virginia took over reef management in the 1970s, and it makes these structures not only from tires, but also from trees, defunct automobiles, brush, rock, concrete, steel, cable, retired New York City subway cars, and old ships. For the most part the reefs hold fast, but between storm action and the natural movement of barrier islands and offshore sediments, disrupted reefs can wreak havoc with Assateague beaches.

The Chincoteague Refuge is one of the top five most visited National Wildlife Refuges in America, with peak visitation between Memorial Day and Labor Day. The town of Chincoteague and Accomack County's major tourist attractions are the Assateague Island recreational beach, the ponies, and the Refuge. The beach lot, now unpaved, has continued to provide parking space for 961 vehicles. Plenty of beach remained for recreational activities such as kite flying, Frisbee tossing, swimming, sunbathing, strolling, and shelling. But for how long?

The National Wildlife Refuge System Administration Act (1966) mandates that each refuge must develop a comprehensive conservation plan (CCP) to guide long-term management of resources, conservation efforts, and public uses and uphold the mission of the refuge system. This plan should be developed with input from the local community and the public at large. Chincoteague NWR implemented its last such plan in the early 1990s.

In December 2011, the Fish and Wildlife Service and Park Service met with representatives from the town of Chincoteague, Accomack County, the National Aeronautics and Space Administration's Wallops Island facility, the state of Virginia, the Accomack-Northampton Planning District Commission, and the Volpe National Transportation Systems Center. Much of the discussion centered on the recreational beach and its parking facilities, off-site beach parking, and an alternative public transportation system. The group fine-tuned the three proposed alternatives.

Alternative A, a "status quo" option, had the Fish and Wildlife Service managing the refuge essentially as it has been run since 1992, with beach access and parking unchanged until the ocean swept it away (USFWS, 2012, p. 1). Alternative B offered compromises such as relocating the recreational beach 1.5 mi/2.4 km to the north on a more stable part of the island near Snow Goose Pool. A and B both includes maintaining the current 961 beach parking spaces. Alternative C prioritized habitat and wildlife management over public use and access, reduced the number of number of parking spaces to 480, and relocated the recreational beach and parking 1.5 mi/2.4 km north of the current beach.

The refuge also considered implementing a voluntary shuttle system to move visitors from off-site locations to the beach and refuge, allowing them to access the beach when the parking lot is full or unusable due to storm damage. The Maddox family of Chincoteague evidently hoped to sell the refuge about 200 acres of land, including the Maddox Family Campground, for off-site beach parking and a staging area for a shuttle system. The price tag for land acquisition alone in 2012 was $7.5 million.

Chincoteague Mayor John Tarr and other local elected officials and business owners have expressed fear that restriction of beach access will cause the economic collapse of the town. Chincoteague is a

Following the July Pony Swim, Saltwater Cowboys drive the ponies though Chincoteague to the fairground. Herd instinct takes over, and the ponies follow one another in a sinuous mass.

gateway community that feeds, lodges, and entertains 1.5 million visitors to the refuge each year.

Visitation to the refuge climbs annually, but the number of resident watermen and their families is dropping. The population of Chincoteague increased from 3,572 to 4,317 between 1990 and 2000, but dropped to 2,941 (-32%) by 2010. Much of the town is empty in the off season—there are almost three times as many housing units as households, 40% of which are made up of people 65 or older. Many of those older residents are retirees from elsewhere. A lot of natives have evidently left the island or turned their former residences into rental properties. Tourism is the economic mainstay of Chincoteague now.

In 2010, the town of Chincoteague conducted a beach access survey of more than 11,500 visitors. Its findings confirmed the fears expressed by some critics. Eighty-two percent of respondents reported that they visited Chincoteague primarily to go to the Assateague beach and that they would not return if the only beach access were by shuttle from an off-island parking area. Many local business owners feared that the Fish and Wildlife Service will develop a parking lot on

Chincoteague

Chincoteague, then fail to maintain onsite beach parking because of environmental and budget concerns.

Moreover, Assateague Island offers the only public beach accessible by automobile in the roughly 100 mi/160 km of coastline between Ocean City, Md., and Virginia Beach, Va. Virtually all of this shorefront is managed by the Fish and Wildlife Service as habitat for waterfowl and other wildlife. Other national parks limit vehicles to public buses. Before Zion National Park in Utah implemented a system of 30 propane-powered shuttle buses, 5,000 private vehicles drove in the park daily. Public transportation has eliminated more than 13,000 tons of greenhouse gas emissions annually. At Acadia National Park in Maine, a propane-powered shuttle bus has eliminated more than 800,000 vehicle trips since 1999.

"We wish to maintain the existing [beach] access and the existing [management] plan as much as possible," said Denise Bowden, whose family has lived on the island for generations (personal communication, February 5, 2011). "We realize the importance of Assateague Island as not only a wildlife refuge but also as a major source of income for Chincoteague Island, and the Eastern Shore as well."

The CCP includes a vision of how the pony herd will be managed 25, 50, 75, and 100 years from now in relation to sea-level rise, wildlife management, and other concerns. This plan is a cooperative effort between the refuge and the fire company, making decisions that will influence future generations of firefighters, park managers, and ponies.

Chincoteaguers live in intimacy with nature's rhythms: the seasons, the tides, the storms and calms, the sowing and growing, the reaping and resting. The firemen have always held to traditional practices, managing the pony herd by drawing from the wisdom of their ancestors to solve problems. They pen ponies in the spring, summer, and fall. In July, they sell the spring foals at auction. The seasons flow from year to year in a comfortable sameness.

Even though the fire company will work with the Fish and Wildlife Service to develop a strategy for pony management, the CCP will impose restrictions on these traditional practices. Local people are concerned about sustaining their traditional way of life and the culture of Chincoteague Island. Unfortunately, traditional lifestyles are often at odds with an evolving world.

Mares and foals snack on marsh grasses after swimming to Chincoteague. Before the early 20th century, there were no spotted horses in the herd. Today, pintos are very popular with visitors and typically fetch the highest prices at auction.

Evidence for global climate change is all around us. The National Academy of Sciences reports that over the past century, the earth's surface temperature has risen by 1.8F°/1C°). The most credible sources predict a global temperature rise 3.2–7.2 F°/1.8– 4.0C° by 2100. The Intergovernmental Panel on Climate Change *Special Report on Emission Scenarios* estimates a possible range of increase of 2.0– 11.5 F°/1.1–6.4C°, depending on the amount of greenhouse gas emissions. NOAA reported that in August 2012, the global temperature exceeded the 20th century average for the 36th consecutive August and 330th consecutive month. Most of this increase has occurred over the past two decades. Montana's Glacier National Park has seen 73% of the area once covered with glacial ice turn to naked rock. By 2030, all of the glaciers in the park may be gone.

Cahill et al. (2012) argue that rising temperatures can cause decline and extinction long before heat itself becomes directly lethal to a species. Among the indirect effects of warming are not only rising sea

After a week of stressful roundups, handling, separation from foals, and the proximity of people, ponies release pent-up anxieties when returned to the refuge, galloping and kicking up their heels.

level, but also changes in salinity, precipitation patterns, vegetation, and fire frequency; harm to beneficial species; benefits to harmful species; and "temporal mismatch between interacting species" (p. 2). As an example of the last-named effect, shorter winters may awaken hibernating animals while plants in their diet that respond to light, not temperature, are still dormant.

When asked what he thought was the most important issue facing the refuge, Hinds answered without hesitation, "Sea level rise." He continued,

> For the last 10,000 years, give or take, sea level has been ris-
> ing. We have enjoyed a very stable period where the rise has
> been slow for the last 3 or 4 thousand years, but it *is* rising.
> If the scientists are correct, that rate of sea level rise will
> increase dramatically over the next 100 years. And that's what
> we are planning for right now. (Personal communication,
> May 21, 2010)

Over the past 3 million years, world average sea level has fluctuated by more than 300 ft/91 m. Over the past 400,000 years, sea level has fallen when glaciers advanced and risen when glaciers melted. About 20,000 years ago, the coast was approximately 62 mi/100 km east of its current location because much of the world's water was locked in the glaciers—the sea-level increase we see today is part of a trend that started at about that time. Sea level rose rapidly until about 6,000 years ago, submerging an older line of islands and pushing sediment deposits up to form the present-day Eastern Seaboard barrier islands. About 3,000 years ago, coastal features struck a balance with the ocean: as the sea level rises and the coastline continues to retreat westward; the barrier islands migrate landward; and the islands, wetlands, lagoons, and other features maintain roughly the same relationships to one another in the absence of interference from humans.

Assateague Island is no more than 46 ft/14 m above sea level at its highest point, and it is extremely vulnerable to changes in sea level. Since Assateague came into existence, oceans have risen about 33 ft/10 m around the world. Global sea level has risen about 7.1 in/18 cm in the last 100 years. In response, the island has gradually migrated up the continental slope through overwash and accretion.

Park Service staff collaborated with the U.S. Geological Survey in 2004 to estimate the sea-level rise and its effects on Assateague. Climate models predict a further rise of 18.9 in/48 cm by 2100, which is more than double the rate of rise for the 20th century. According to the 2007 National Parks Conservation Association assessment, sea level is rising 0.124 in/3.15 mm annually, but may increase by a factor of 2–5 in the next century, enough to overwhelm the island's ability to adjust. Interestingly, the Atlantic coast from Cape Hatteras to Massachusetts appears to experience sea-level rise 3–4 times higher than the global average, possibly due to oceanic currents, plate tectonics, and gravitational changes influenced by icemelt.

Barrier islands respond to accelerated sea-level rise by becoming narrower. Thinning allows for frequent cross-island overwash that permits these islands to migrate quickly and efficiently in step with sea-level rise. With climate change comes increasingly violent storms, which accelerate overwash, erosion, inlet formation, and other processes. Farther south, the narrower parts of North Carolina's Outer Banks could disappear entirely.

Rising sea level affects all aspects of the Chincoteague NWR—loss of wildlife habitat, shoreline erosion, inundation of wetlands, saltwater intrusion into estuaries and freshwater aquifers, and damage to cultural and historic resources and infrastructure. As climate change raises the water temperature, algae blooms may increase in estuarine waters, decreasing water quality and stressing aquatic grasses and fish communities.

Hinds said (personal communication, May 21, 2010),

> At first, people will want to fight Mother Nature, putting up barriers against sea level rise, because they will want to protect their homes, their business, or their way of life. They don't want to change the way they have always lived, but change is inevitable and nature will have her way in the end.

Using a computerized Sea Level Affecting Marsh Model (SLAMM) analysis, Delissa Padilla Nieves showed that if sea level rose 1 m by the year 2100, 57% of the salt marsh would be swallowed by the sea, including most of the grazing area within the southern compartment. Grazing appears to accelerate this loss by reducing or eliminating the accumulation of detritus necessary for salt marsh root systems to keep pace with rising sea levels.

Grazed marshes have a lower profile and may be more prone to flooding as sea level rises. A study involving feral horse grazing in the Rachel Carson National Estuarine Research Reserve in North Carolina observed that grazed marshes showed sparser growth of *Spartina* grasses, with decreased cover, blade length, and seed production, and a decrease in sediment buildup. Chincoteague NWR is using a projection of 3.3 ft/1 m of sea-level rise over the next 100 years. That figure has dramatic implications for wildlife management and visitor services. Hinds said that within the next 50 years, the south corral area will be too wet to support ponies, and large portions of the present marsh will be open water.

In fact, after a series of nor'easters slammed the East Coast in January, 2011, a number of ponies were moved from the flooded pasture to the north end of the refuge. The north end is higher, contains more acreage, and has more varied terrain. Although that area may also be reduced by sea-level rise, it will probably remain adequate for pony habitat. If rising sea level significantly decreases the size of the island, Hinds said that the number of Chincoteague Ponies permitted in the refuge will need to decrease correspondingly to remain in balance with the ecosystem (personal communication, May 21, 2010). The Fish and Wildlife Service recommends, but does not demand, that the fire company maintain the herd at 134 adult ponies or fewer until the year 2023, when stakeholders will consider updated climate-change data.

Currently, the refuge uses intentional disturbances within the impoundments to enhance the habitat for migrating birds. Wintering waterfowl benefit from the cutting of emergent vegetation—the plants that grow in water but extend above the surface. Resource managers sometimes mow, disc with tractors, or set fires to reduce vegetation and allow sunlight to reach the ground.

In the future, refuge managers may enlist the help of willing conspirators—the Chincoteague Ponies—to create such disturbances. Utilizing Chincoteague Ponies in the management of impoundments would reduce the use of staff, tractors, and fuel. Grazing ponies could clear away undergrowth and punch in seed with their hooves. Their waste, broken down by invertebrates and microorganisms, could help sustain the small creatures on which shorebirds feed.

Research has validated the benefits of using horse grazing to manage estuarine habitats. In managing habitat for waterfowl, grazing encourages a diverse assortment of plants and reduces woody vegetation in moist soil areas. Planned rest periods between intervals of grazing allow tall grass cover to reestablish itself for waterfowl nesting. Land that has been grazed develops a patchy herb layer that is desirable habitat for some birds. Despite its inflexible stance against grazing, elsewhere in the country, the Fish and Wildlife Service has advocated grazing to create desirable habitat for Attwater's prairie chickens. And in the Virginia mountains, the U.S. Forest Service introduced Shetland ponies in 1974 to reduce overgrowth on Mt. Rogers and the Grayson Highlands.

There is good evidence that grazing by horses on barrier islands increases the population of small crabs, which in turn attract diverse species of waterfowl. Wigeon, gadwall, and pochard feed on submerged plants that grow better when the marsh is grazed. Horse grazing in the Camargue of France has proved useful for management of marshes for waterfowl by opening up the emergent vegetation, especially where the water level is controlled by the manager.

The invasive *Phragmites* reed is nutritious and palatable to horses, and grazing pressures weaken its unwanted foothold on estuarine margins. When *Phragmites* shoots are bitten off below water level, the plant often starts to decompose and may die. Under heavy grazing

Phragmites declines quickly in height and density. *Phragmites* grows tall and dense in ungrazed exclosures, but it is low and sparse in heavily grazed areas. Herbicides and regular grazing may be the only things that can kill *Phragmites*, and the latter is much less destructive.

On the Chincoteague Refuge, the ponies are abundant and not at all shy of visitors, but they are confined behind barbed wire, which keeps them off the pavement and away from people. Visitors can view ponies with binoculars from the observation platform on the Woodland Trail or across the roadside fences, but the animals are often distant.

The federal agencies charged with managing feral horses on Assateague have philosophical differences regarding interaction between the American public and wild equids. The Fish and Wildlife Service claims it puts distance between people and ponies on the Chincoteague refuge "to keep the wildness in the animals" (L. Hinds, personal communication, May 21, 2010), an unusual stance for an agency that does not classify them as wildlife. More likely, the separation is imposed to prevent injuries and lawsuits—and perhaps to prevent the public from forming stronger attachments to the ponies and advocating for their retention.

The Park Service allows horses to remain in certain parks, such as Cape Hatteras NS, as a cultural resource, and manages them as wildlife on Assateague Island, Cape Lookout, and Cumberland Island National Seashores, in Theodore Roosevelt National Park, and at other sites even though it officially classifies them as feral livestock. While prohibiting direct contact, Assateague National Seashore and Assateague State Park on the Maryland end of the island allow ponies to roam freely into areas where people congregate.

Visitors can see the northern part of the Chincoteague NWR by walking the 8-mi/12.8-km service road or by taking a guided bus tour operated during the summer months by the Chincoteague Natural History Association, a nonprofit organization that works with the Fish and Wildlife Service in providing educational opportunities. A number of Chincoteague watermen offer scenic boat cruises to watch ponies and other wildlife on Assateague at close range.

People tapped Assateague's resources long before any records were kept. Paleo-Indians probably foraged along the East Coast and its islands for thousands of years, but we have little evidence of their

A mare reassures her frightened foal that he is safe, even as her own nervousness shows in her expression. Tomorrow, however, the fire company will abruptly wean him and separate him from his mother forever. While the first day or two apart is stressful for both, all foals must leave their mothers at some time.

presence, nor are we likely to find much useful information about them. Sea level has risen considerably since these early inhabitants took up residence. The land where they lived was swallowed by the ocean, by westward-moving estuaries, or by the migrating barrier chain, and in some cases may be 200 mi/322 km out to sea on the continental shelf. Archaic tools are sometimes found in the sand dredged from offshore bars and piped onto Ocean City beaches, but out of context they reveal few insights.

Before Europeans arrived, various native tribes of the Algonquian linguistic family used the island seasonally for hunting and fishing. The Chincoteague Indians lived not on Chincoteague, but on the mainland, alongside a number of native tribes who named themselves after the creeks on which they lived, or vice versa. Popular tradition and nearly every guidebook describing the island hold that *Chincoteague* translates to "beautiful land across the water." Kirk Mariner writes (2003, p.4) that it actually means "large stream or inlet." Similarly, Dunbar notes a possible etymological connection between Chincoteague and Ginguite Creek on the northern Outer Banks. The 1651/1667 Farrer map, below, shows "Cingoto" as a specific island.

The Chincoteague Indians lived in settlements on the mainland and migrated seasonally to barrier islands to make use of food sources. Their villages were located where they were sheltered from storms, above the reach of the tides, and near freshwater. These natives visited Chincoteague and Assateague islands to forage for shellfish, fish, and game and to collect shells used to make beads, which they used as currency.

In the early 1500s, Spain explored the East Coast as far north as South Carolina while England had explored at least as far south as Nova Scotia. The first recorded European to set foot on Maryland or Virginia was an Italian named Giovanni da Verrazzano, who sailed for the King Francis I of France in 1524 aboard a ship named *La Dauphine*. Some historians believe that he may have landed on or near Assateague Island. Others place his landing at about 10 mi/16 km north of Cape Charles. He named his find "Arcadia," which he described as "beautiful and full of the largest forests" (Covington, 1915, p. 205).

His was not a welcome landing. Verrazzano wrote in his letter to the king that the first person his party encountered was a man, "handsome, nude, with hair fastened back in a knot, of olive color," who extended a burning stick to the party "as if to offer us fire" in what was probably a friendly gesture (Covington, 1915, p. 207). Verrazzano's crew responded with fire of its own. "We made fire with powder and flint-and-steel, and he trembled all over with terror, and we fired a shot. He stopped as if astonished and prayed, worshipping like a monk, lifting his finger toward the sky, and pointing to the ship and sea, he appeared to bless us" (Covington, 1915, p. 207).

European explorers often abducted native children so that they might learn the language of their captors, convert to Christianity, and act as interpreters and mediators in converting their people. English colonists also left their own boys in Indian villages to learn the native language. Verrazzano describes successfully kidnapping an 8-year-old native boy to take back to France. He wrote of his unsuccessful attempt to abduct a teenage girl "of much beauty and tall of stature, but it was not possible on account of the very great cries which she uttered for us to conduct her to the sea" (Wise, 1911, p. 6). The Spanish abducted children as well, taking a boy from the Potomac River area and another from the Eastern Shore in 1588.

Verrazzano describes the natives as lighter-skinned than those he had previously seen. They clothed themselves in Spanish moss (which can still be found hanging from cypress trees along the Pocomoke River), hunted, fished from dugout canoes, and ate wild peas. Their arrows were made from reeds with tips fashioned from bone.

There were about 2,000 Native Americans on the Eastern Shore in 1608, including the Pocomoke, Annamessex, Manokin, Nassawattex, Acquintica, Assateague, Chincoteague, and Kickotank. These tribes are represented in the historical record as "timid, harmless, kind-hearted people" (Upshur, 1901, p. 91). It is unlikely that any of these tribes lived on the barrier islands year-'round because of insufficient game, poor soil, and horrendous storms.

In September 1649, Henry Norwood and 329 other colonists left England bound for Jamestown aboard the *Virginia Merchant*. After three wretched months at sea, Norwood and a dozen of the sickest men and women went ashore on a Delmarva barrier island to find drinking water. They were abandoned on the isolated beach in the dead of winter when their ship left without them! Historians dispute the location where Norwood was stranded, but evidence suggests that it was Assateague or Assawoman Island.

They had little ammunition, but managed to feed themselves on oysters and game birds. When Norwood sent his cousin to look for friendly Indians, he realized that he and his party were on a barrier island far from the mainland villages. One by one, members of the group died of cold, exposure, and hunger, and the rest survived by turning to cannibalism. Certainly if horses or other livestock had been on the island when Norwood arrived, his party would have eaten them rather than one another, or at least he would have mentioned them. Wild game was also scarce and elusive—Verrazzano had commented that "the animals in these regions are wilder than in Europe from being continually molested by the hunters," and deer were uncommon (Langley et al., 2009). Norwood was about to try swimming to the mainland to seek help from the local tribes when on the ninth or 10th day, they were rescued by Kickotanks.

The Indians showed them great hospitality and dispatched a messenger who brought back Jenkin Price, a fur trader, to accompany them to the nearest English settlement. They traveled on foot for a day and lodged with the Chincoteague tribe overnight in their home on the mainland, and Norwood woke in the morning to find the chief's daughter sharing his bed, a gesture of hospitality from his hosts. During their stay with the natives, Norwood and company feasted on oysters, deer, duck, goose, curlew, and swan—a veritable bounty of game and seafood obtained from the same environs where Norwood's party nearly starved. "The shore swarmed with fowl," he wrote, and the Indians told him that wolves "'did greatly abound in that island'" (Covington, 1915, p. 213).

When Europeans began to settle the Choptank River watershed on the Eastern Shore of Maryland, only about 2% of the region was cleared by the local Native people; 92%–94% of the landscape was forest and about 6% wetlands. By setting periodic forest fires, the Natives maintained open woodland with minimal underbrush to obstruct their passage. Native people typically lived in rectangular homes made of perishable local materials with the capacity to house about 20 individuals. When the group relocated seasonally to access food sources or moved to till new ground, their belongings went with them, leaving little enduring to mark where the village once stood.

Initially, interactions between settlers and the Native people were amicable, centering on trading for corn in Virginia and for furs in Maryland. The Eastern Shore tribes did not participate in the Jamestown massacre of March 1622, so relations between settlers and natives remained guarded but friendly.

Settlers obtained Indian lands through purchase, trade, or patenting apparently abandoned lands, ignoring laws passed in 1652, 1654, and 1658 to regulate and limit acquisition of land by Europeans. By the 1650s, natives were losing rights to residential lands as well as to hunting grounds and areas used for agriculture.

As Europeans grabbed more territory, relations with the natives soured. When rumors circulated that the natives were plotting to poison the wells of the settlers, Edmund Scarborough, infamous for

Ponies return to Assateague in July to resume a wild existence until October, when the Saltwater Cowboys will gather them for inspection and routine care.

his fanatical hatred of all Indians, repeatedly incited conflict against them, a penchant that led to his prosecution in Jamestown. In 1651, he led a brutal attack on the Pocomoke tribe, which served to increase resentment toward whites and strengthen cohesion among tribes.

In 1659, backed by the governor of Virginia, but not that of Maryland, Scarborough descended on the peaceful Assateague tribe with 300 men and 60 horses. The Assateagues could not have been numerous, because they were described as "harder to find than to conquer" (Langley & Jordan, 2007, p. 19). His intention was to ensure that the tribe "may neither plant corne, hunt, or fish, soe make him poore and famish him" (Mariner, 2003, p. 10). Later called the Seaside War of 1659, this encounter weakened the tribe, and thereafter it shrank in population and in territory. In 1660, the Indians of Accomack complained that they had lost so much land that they could not survive.

The Delmarva Indians may already have been in decline by the time permanent settlers arrived from Europe. In the summer of 1608, John Smith reported that the Accomack had recently suffered a "strange mortalitie" (1624, p. 55). Some researchers have suggested that they succumbed to a European disease, perhaps smallpox or influenza, from earlier contacts.

Conflict, disease, and flight removed many Indians from the landscape. Assimilation, poor documentation, lost or destroyed papers, and the advantages of passing for white removed many of the survivors from the historical record. The final blow to many Virginia Indians may have been the Racial Integrity Act of 1924, a result of the eugenics movement, which reduced the list of officially recognized racial identities to two: white and colored. The Act mandated that officials record the race of every person at birth using the "one drop" rule—anyone with African or Native American ancestry, no matter how remote, was classed as colored, and as such was excluded from white schools and forbidden to marry a white. The First Families of Virginia, a lineage society comprising descendants of the original Virginia colonists, including Pocahontas, protested. The "Pocahontas exemption" granted white status to anyone less than 1/8 Indian.

The boundary between Maryland and Virginia was established in 1668, and within a few decades European settlers had claimed "every foot of the territory from the Western shore of Smiths Island, in the Chesapeake bay, to the Eastern shore of Assateague island, on the Atlantic Ocean, on the whole course of the divisional line run by Calvert and Scarbrough" (Virginia Commission on Boundary Lines, 1873, p. 133).

In 1667, a sailor with smallpox wandered into an Indian village and succeeded in spreading the disease all along the Eastern Shore, devastating the native population. The native tribes believed this sailor had been sent among them by the whites to kill them. Whether or not this was true, the effect was the same. (There is a satisfying irony in reports that Scarborough himself also died of smallpox.)

Wise (1911, p. 66) wrote,

> The peaceful Indians of the Eastern Shore, among whom the first colonists of the peninsula had settled, had greatly diminished by the end of the 17th century, and the dying out of the Savages was followed by the arrival of Negroes in large numbers, of whom up to that time there had been but few.

He also describes the first horse on Virginia's Eastern Shore as one conveyed to Colonel Argoll Yeardley by George Ludlow of the Western Shore by a bill of sale dated January 30th 1642. None of the many inventories on record prior to that date includes horses. . . . In 1645 Stephen Charlton also owned a horse and in November of that year a consignment of horses

The corrals bring mature stallions into close proximity, and dramatic battles often flare. Witch Doctor (left) and half-Arabian Copper Moose (right) were so intent on combat, the water troughs were no obstacle. Copper Moose was a 1996 Buyback, claiming the highest bid in the auction at $5,000.

arrived from New England, many of the animals having died on the passage south. The custom of branding stock was begun at this time. (1911, p. 307)

Wise considered it unlikely that the wild horse herds of Assateague had arrived by shipwreck ahead of the colonists, commenting that if the horses had been on these islands, early settlers would have made use of them. He writes (1911, p. 308),

> When Chincoteague Island was first prospected and granted to one of the colonists in 1670 by James II no mention of horses occurs. Again while Colonel Norwood, who was shipwrecked on the nearby coast and spent some time in the neighborhood as the guest of the hospitable Kickotanke chieftain, mentions the presence of large numbers of hogs in the marshes near Gingo Teague, he does not mention horses. Colonel Norwood passed right by the island in 1649 and would certainly have mentioned the wild horses had they been there at that time. It has also been said that the wild ponies which rove in great herds over the Accomac island owe their origin to horses left there by pirates in the early days but this too is doubtful . . . the number of horses in the colony in 1631 was very small and prior to 1649 references in the records of Virginia to horses are exceedingly rare.

Horses were scarce in the earliest Virginia settlements. John Smith wrote that in the fall of 1609 nearly 500 colonists at Jamestown had "fiue or sixe hundred Swine; as many Hennes and Chickens; some Goats; some sheepe," but only "six Mares and a Horse" (1624, p. 93). Although recent scholarship suggests that salty drinking water (made saltier by prolonged drought) and poor sanitation may have killed many people, hunger was severe and drove a few to cannibalism. After the winter of 1610, the infamous "starving time," just 60 colonists remained alive. Livestock fared worse. "As for our Hogs, Hens, Goats, Sheepe, Horse, or what liued," Smith wrote, "our commanders, officers & Saluages daily consumed them . . . till all was deuoured" (1624, p. 105).

The suffering and desperation of the settlers were evident in George Percy's account:

> Haveinge fedd [upon] horses and other beastes as longe as they Lasted, we weare gladd to make shifte w[i]th vermin as

A 2005 buckskin mare, Kachina Grand Star, grazes in the marsh of the north pasture shortly after Pony Penning week. She is probably pregnant with next year's foal—on Chincoteague NWR, most mares foal annually.

doggs Catts Ratts and myce . . . to eate Bootes shoes or any other leather. . . . notheinge was Spared to mainteyne Lyfe and to doe those things w[hi]ch seame incredible, as to digge upp deade corpes outt of graves and to eate them. . . . one of our Colline murdered his wyfe Ripped the Childe outt of her woambe and threwe itt into the River and after Chopped the Mother in pieces and sallted her for his foode. (Percy, 1625, p. 7)

The meat from butchered livestock meant survival for individual colonists, but to survive as a colony, Jamestown needed breeding stock. The horses were replaced in the spring of 1611, when Sir Thomas Dale brought 17 stallions and mares. In 1612, Virginia's deputy governor, Sir Thomas Gates, made it a capital crime to kill "any Bull, Cow, Calfe, Mare, Horse, Colt, Goate, Swine, Cocke, Henne, Chicken, Dogge, Turkie, or any tame Cattel, or Poultry, of what condition soever" without permission (Anderson, 2002, p. 381).

In October 1613 Captain Samuel Argall (who had kidnapped the famed Pocahontas in April of that year) sailed 500 miles to Port Royal, Nova Scotia, destroyed the French settlement, and absconded with whatever he could use, including a number of horses. Sources differ on how these horses had reached Canada. One says that "In 1604, M. L'Escarbot, a French lawyer, brought several horses to Acadia. From this stock sprung the famous Canada ponies, which, owing to the bitter climate in which they live, do not represent the size of their Norman ancestors, but are still the knottiest, naughtiest, hardiest little creatures of their kind in the world" (Washburn, 1877, p. 379). Others say that King Henry IV of France had supplied them and that they were probably similar to the horses sent to Quebec in 1665 by Louis XIV from his royal stables in Normandy and Brittany. The Quebec horses were to become the foundation stock for the rugged Canadian Horse breed, carrying Spanish, Barb, and Arabian bloodlines infused with the draft blood of the Breton and the French Norman.

The horses Argall brought to Jamestown were probably representative of the finest French bloodlines of the time. This importation is another means by which Spanish genes might have reached the horses of colonial Virginia without direct introduction by the Spanish, who tended to take southern routes to the New World. It is unclear, however, whether any of the Canadian horses survived to contribute their genes to the Virginia colonial stock.

Until 1624, the Virginia Company was the principal source for imported livestock to the colonies. Ralph Hamor noted the presence of horses in his *True Discourse on the Present State of Virginia* (1615, cited in Wallace, 1897, p. 109), "The colony is already furnished with two hundred neat cattle, infinite hogs in herds all over the woods, some mares, horses and colts, poultry, etc." A census in 1620, though, counted only eleven horses in the colony. The Virginia Company sent out 20 English mares later that year to bolster the breeding herd. Sir Francis Wyatt reported in 1626 that more horses were needed for military purposes and for the manufacture of pitch and tar. The equine population was to grow very slowly—almost 30 years later, there were still only about 200 horses in Virginia.

The colonists of the Chesapeake Bay region initially imported all the livestock typically found on English farms, but over time the barnyard census shifted to reflect local conditions. Sheep were impractical because of predation, so wool and mutton were scarce until the end of the 17th century, when many predators had been eradicated.

Historian and novelist Edward Eggleston points out another obstacle to sheep raising:

> The only domestic animal that did not multiply to excess in the wild pastures of America was the sheep, which had for deadly foes the American wolf and the English woolen manufacturer. . . . There was nothing that English legislation of the time sought more persistently than the development of the English woolen trade. . . . the importation of a sheep for the improvement of the colonial breed was punishable with the amputation of the right hand. (1884, pp. 445–446)

Encouraged by generous bounties, stockmen eliminated predators, but were otherwise inattentive to their free-range flocks. "The negligent methods prevalent in a new country bore more hardly on sheep than on other animals, and it was estimated that about one-third of all the sheep in the northern colonies perished in a single hard winter, a little before the middle of the eighteenth century" (Eggleston, 1884, p. 446).

Following the lead of the Indians, farmers raised tobacco and corn largely with hoes, not plows; so few oxen were needed, and horses were generally not used for plowing.

Between 1637 and 1777, Virginia colonists practiced "open-woodlands husbandry," allowing animals to range freely. The major cash crop was tobacco, and by allowing the livestock to range freely in the woods and fields the settlers reaped maximal animal production with minimal labor, freeing the men to work in labor-intensive tobacco cultivation. Colonists also used the woods as a way to avoid paying taxes on animals, a problem addressed by the Virginia statutes in 1646: "such persons who have concealed the number of their persons tithable, lands, horses, mares & c. shall for every tithable person, lands, & c. pay double the rate that this present Grand Assembly hath assessed" (Hening, 1823, vol. 1, p. 329).

Unfortunately the free-roaming animals did not differentiate between what they were supposed to eat and what was forbidden to them, and they often destroyed crops. In 1643, the Virginia Assembly ruled that colonists had to fence in their crops, not their animals. Three years later, Assembly required crop fencing to be 4.5 ft/1.4 m high (subsequently increased to 5 ft/1.5 m) and "substantiall close downe to the bottome" (Hening, 1823, vol. 1, p. 332). In other words, the barrier was to be tall enough that horses were unlikely to jump it and low enough to thwart rooting pigs. Those who did not enclose their crops would "plant, uppon theire owne perill" (Hening, 1823, vol. 1, p. 199).

The landscape of the English colonies functioned as a vast grazing commons for unsupervised livestock, with fenced patches of tobacco and corn surrounded by large open meadows and forest. For the next 250 years, fencing laws in many states followed this model; cultivators were responsible for fencing their crops and had no recourse if free-roaming livestock invaded their fields.

In 1649, there were 200 documented horses in the colony, 20,000 head of cattle, 50 asses, 3,000 sheep, 5,000 goats, "innumerable" swine, and poultry "without number" (Farrer, 1649, p. 3). In the late 1660s, the Assembly first repealed its prohibition of exporting horses, then forbade their importation "to restraine the numerous increase of horses now rather growing burthensome then any way advantagious to the country" (Hening, 1823, vol. 2, pp. 267, 271).

Farrer (1649, p. 3) describes Virginia horses as "of an excellent raise [race]." Thomas Glover (1676, cited in Harrison, 1927, p. 332) pronounced Virginia's horses to be "as good as we have in England." John Clayton, parson of Jamestown, wrote to the Royal Society (1688, cited in Harrison, p. 332),

> There are good store of Horses, though they are very negligent and careless about the breed. It is true there is a law that no Horse shall be kept stoned [uncastrated] under a certain size, but it is not put in Execution. Such as they are there are good stock, and as cheap or cheaper than in England, worth

about five pounds apiece. They never shoe them nor stable them in general.

In *Un Français en Virginie* (1687, cited in Harrison, 1927, p. 332), Durand commented,

> I do not believe there are better horses in the world, or worse treated. All the care they take of them at the end of a journey is to unsaddle, feed a little Indian corn and so, all covered with sweat, drive them out into the woods, where they eat what they can find, even though it is freezing.

In the late 1600s colonial cattle and horses alike were denied shelter even in extremes of weather and were expected to forage for themselves in all seasons. Sometimes they survived a harsh winter by eating the bark from trees. Perhaps as a result, English livestock apparently matured to a smaller size when raised free-range in the Chesapeake area. Wild stallions stole mares in heat or made forays into the plantations to breed with them. Colonists complained that random mating "'doth both Lessen & spoyle the whole breed and Streyne of all horses'" (Anderson, 2002, p. 403).

Nobody really knew how many domestic animals roamed Virginia during colonial times. Robert Beverley wrote in the early 1700s, "Hogs swarm like Vermine upon the Earth, and . . . find their own Support in the Woods, without any Care of the Owner" (1705, p. 81). He added (p. 76), "the wild Horses are so swift, that 'tis difficult to catch them; and when they are taken . . . they are so sullen, that they can't be tam'd." To increase horses' stature, in 1686 the Virginia legislature forbade planters to turn into the woods "any ston'd [uncastrated] horse two years old or more and under thirteen and one-half hands" (Harrison, 1927, p. 332).

As the number of English planters increased, so did the number of livestock roaming the country and destroying the unfenced crops of local Indians. Frustrated by shrinking hunting grounds and the depredations of ravenous livestock, the Assateague tribe staged a minor and fruitless raid on white settlements in 1659. Surviving records do not clarify how this event was related to the Seaside War of the same year.

By 1669, there were so many semi-wild horses in Virginia that further importation was prohibited and stallions were to be gelded if caught. Planters even shipped surplus animals to Barbados and New

England. Laws were passed requiring horse owners to reimburse farmers for damaged crops and fences, but there were many horses—some without owners—and crops were under constant assault.

Through the early 1700s, horse owners sometimes employed various devices to keep horses close to home and out of the fields. A horse lock, a piece of wood fastened between the fore and hind legs of the horse, prevented the animal from galloping or leaping. Hobbles were created by tying the horse's neck to a hind fetlock. Some owners used a modified yoke with a hook on the bottom that would catch on the top rail of a fence if a horse tried to jump it.

When tobacco prices collapsed in the late 1600s, the settlers compensated by growing wheat and keeping sheep. Free-range horses became such a nuisance, young men hunted them with dogs for sport—though it appears the object was capturing, not killing, the horses. A planter could shoot horses found depredating his crops. In 1662, a tax was levied on horses, and owners were required to keep them confined from July 20 until October 20. As marauding livestock grew more vexing, laws were passed demanding that all livestock be fenced, and anyone who captured unbranded free-roaming livestock gained legal ownership of them.

As early as 1657, Virginia colonists circumvented the maze of disputes, laws, and taxes and avoided the expensive trouble of fencing by turning their stock loose on nearby islands. In the late 1600s, wealthy landowners of the Eastern Shore acquired many islands on the coast and in Chesapeake Bay for this purpose; Saxis, Watts, Tangier, Smith, Hog, Assateague, Chincoteague, Parramore, Metompkin, and Wallops islands were all put to use grazing hogs, goats, sheep, cattle, and horses by the end of the 17th century. Owners singly or jointly put their livestock on necks and barrier islands to forage without endangering crops and survive at minimal expense.

Captain Daniel Jenifer held the first patents on both Chincoteague Island (1671) and the Virginia part of Assateague Island (1687). The Maryland part of Assateague was not patented until the 1700s.

In *Harper's Monthly* novelist, professor, and children's author Maude Radford Warren wrote,

> Some of the islanders vigorously oppose the tradition that Chincoteague was originally settled by convicts, but the evidence tends in that direction. In the old days a planter was

Descendants of the original settlers still gather descendants of the original ponies in the shadow of the Assateague Light. This tradition has persisted for hundreds of years with little change.

allowed fifty acres of land for each settler he introduced. In 1687 Captain Daniel Jenifer brought over a number of convicts, perhaps seven, perhaps thirty-five, and in return Chincoteague and Assoteague [sic] were patented to him. Twice the patent of Chincoteague lapsed, but finally, in 1692, twenty-five hundred acres of the lower half were given to John Robbins and twenty-five hundred of the upper half to Col. William Kendall, and from these two men almost all the people now on the island got their titles (1913, p. 775)

Thomas Welburn and his four employees were the first white settlers on Chincoteague Island, arriving in 1680 to "seat" the island by building a house and planting tobacco, apple trees, and corn (Mariner, 2003). Welburn's tenant, Robert Scott, was probably the first white man to live on the island—for the year required by law to cement Welburn's claim to the island. When Edward Hammond visited Chincoteague in 1681, he found that the crops had gone wild, and the local natives were enjoying the use of both the house and the corn.

Records are vague, but livestock seems to have been present on Assateague since the late 1600s. If the present-day horses of

Chincoteague

Assateague descend from this population, they can boast more than three centuries of continuous occupancy. By 1684 the Welburn claim was considered abandoned, and it wound up in the possession of William Kendall, an affluent and influential slave-owner. Welburn, believing himself the rightful owner of Chincoteague Island, threatened to shoot Kendall if he dared "seat" there himself. Nonetheless, Kendall went to the island with Major John Robins and Thomas Eyre and erected "a small house . . . about ten foot long like ye roof of a house upon ye ground" (Mariner, 2003, p. 13). Welburn fought the claim in court, but in 1691, the general court awarded half of the island to Kendall and half to Major Robins. The dividing line was near modern-day Church Street. Chincoteague was on its way to becoming a town.

Chincoteague had little arable land, but like most of the barrier islands of the Eastern Shore, it was ideally suited for raising livestock. Horses, cattle, goats, hogs, and sheep roamed freely in the late 1600s. Robins's will, recorded May 28, 1709, bequeathed to his sons his land on "Jingoteague island . . . where my man and woman George and Hannah Blake look after the stock" (Mariner, 2003, p. 18). Another heir received a horse from the livestock grazed on "Gingoteague Island," indicating that horses roamed the island at that time (Mariner, 2003, p. 18). (*Chincoteague* is spelled three different ways in this document alone—spellings of English and Indian names did not become fixed until much later.)

Through the 1700s, the names of the wealthy absentee landowners appear on record, but it was the tenants that lived and worked on the island, and their names were often lost to history. Oral tradition maintains that early settlers often intermarried with Native Americans. Mariner describes simple homes—one-story windowless frame buildings with sand floors and a hole cut in the ceiling to let smoke escape from the primitive fireplace—but some of these dwellings may have been seasonal. Light was provided by fish oil burned in clam shells.

Warren wrote about a later period, the mid-19th century, and offered a different description of local architecture:

> In those early days they had log houses a story and a half in height, boarded outside, plastered inside, and supported on great cedar blocks. Most of the houses had great hearths

which would hold logs as large as a man, and fine brick chimneys; the poorer people, however, had "andiron" chimneys made of lime and laths. In 1840 there were about five hundred people living in twenty-six houses. They did not build more, for in those times the young people would "win away" to Delaware and Pennsylvania. (1913, p. 782)

DeVincent Hayes and Bennett published an old photograph of Kendall Jester's sturdy residence, purportedly constructed in 1727. It had front steps and a masonry chimney, and it was substantial enough to form the nucleus of the Lighthouse Inn, which stood till the 1960s.

In 1776, the Virginia Convention ordered livestock removed from the Eastern Shore islands to prevent British ships from raiding them as a food source. At that time, Chincoteague was home to 20 families plus horses, cattle, and about 400 sheep; more livestock ran free on Assateague. The islanders petitioned to keep the livestock on the islands, stating that they had themselves organized a militia and a guard of 30–40 men stationed in the area and would bear the loss themselves if they could not protect their livestock from "'small cruising vessels of the enemy'" (Force, 1846, p. 1563). The Convention rescinded its order.

Dr. Thompson Holmes owned a mainland plantation on Chincoteague Bay and built a home on the island in 1811. Almost 25 years later, as he departed from the island, he wrote in eloquent detail about the local horses and their habitat (1835, p. 418):

> Assateague and Chincoteague islands are flat, sandy and soft, producing abundance of excellent grass, upon which they become very fat during the summer and autumn, notwithstanding the annoyance of flies, with which those islands frequently abound. . . .
>
> Their winter subsistence was supplied abundantly by nature. The tall, dense, and heavy grass of the rich flat lands, affording them green food nearly the whole winter, the tops of which alone were killed by the frosts, mild, as usual, so near the ocean. They never suffered for provender, except in very deep snows, with a crust upon the top, or when high tides were immediately succeeded by intense cold, which covered the marsh pastures with ice, both of which accidents were of rare occurrence, and very transient in their duration.

He added (1835, p. 419),

> They are hardy, rarely affected with the diseases to which the horse is subject, perform a great deal of labor, if proportioned to their strength, require much less grain than common horses, live long, and are, many of them, delightful for the saddle. I have a beautiful island pony, who for fifteen years has been my riding nag in the neighborhood and upon the farm, who has given to my daughters their first lessons in equestrian exercise, and has carried us all many thousands of miles in pleasure and safety, without having once tripped or stumbled; and he is now as elastic in his gait, and juvenile in his appearance, as he was the first day I backed him, and is fatter than any horse I own, though his labor is equal, with less than two-thirds of their grain consumption. His eye still retains its good natured animation, and to one unskilled in the indications of a horse's teeth, he would pass readily for six or seven years old. My regrets at parting with this noble little animal, are those of the friend.

Nearly 200 years ago, this educated observer saw nothing unusual about these horses except their diminutive size and greater stamina. He supports the idea that all Delmarva horses—island and mainland—originated from the same colonial stock and discredits the shipwreck hypothesis:

> In regard to the origin of the race of our insular horses, there is no specific difference between them and those of the main land: the smaller size and superior hardihood of the former are entirely accidental, produced by penury of sustenance through the winter, occasional scarcity of water, continual exposure to the inclemency of the seasons, and the careless practice of permitting promiscuous copulation among them, without regard to quality. (Holmes, 1835, p. 418)

He concluded that little effort would be needed to bring these horses up to their ancestors' stature:

> The largest and finest work-steers of the Eastern Shore, are raised upon these islands, without any expenditure for winter support; a proof that horses of full size, might also be reared there, with judicious attention to the breed, proper selection of stallions, and care to provide water. No other attention is

necessary, except to watch the winds and weather about the periods of the equinoxes, when desolating tides are threatened, and to drive the stock upon high grounds, secure against inundation. (Holmes, 1835, p. 419)

Two decades later, Charles Lanman (1856, p. 235) wrote of Assateague,

From time immemorial it has been famous for its luxuriant grass, and from the period of the Revolution down to the year 1800, supplied an immense number of wild horses with food. When the animals were first introduced upon the island has not been ascertained, but it is said that they were most abundant half a century ago. At that period there was a kind of stock company in existence, composed principally of the wealthier planters residing on the main shore. The animals were of the pony breed, but generally beautifully formed and very fleet, of a deep black color, and with remarkably long tails and manes. They lived and multiplied on the island without the least care from the hand of man, and though feeding entirely on the grass of the salt meadows, they were in good condition throughout the year. They were employed by their owners, to a considerable extent, for purposes of agriculture, but the finer specimens were kept or disposed of as pets for the use of ladies and children. The prices which they commanded on the island varied from ten to twenty dollars [about $250–500 today], but by the time a handsome animal could reach New York or New Orleans, he was likely to command one hundred and fifty or two hundred dollars [roughly $3,800–5,000].

These ponies were solid-colored—bays, blacks, and sorrels. An account from 1897 says, "They are about thirteen hands high, uniform in shape, and resemble each other except in color, for all colors prevail" (Wallace, p. 111). A comfortable pacing gait (legs moving in lateral pairs rather than the diagonal pairs of the trot) or a four-beat amble was desirable in Colonial days. Horses were chiefly used to carry a rider long distances along unimproved trails. Hugh Jones (1724/1865, p. 49) wrote that the Virginia horse "will pace naturally and pleasantly at a prodigious rate." Like their brethren on the mainland, some of the horses of Chincoteague and Assateague also paced.

A "gaited" horse naturally performs a smooth four-beat amble, running walk, or singlefoot gait. Modern horses such as the Paso Fino, Peruvian Paso, Tennessee Walking Horse, Rocky Mountain Horse, and Missouri Fox Trotter are gaited, and this characteristic is common in breeds with old Spanish lineage. Spanish Jennets apparently also carried the genes for the two-beat pace, as demonstrated by modern Standardbreds and the extinct Narragansett Pacers.

In the Chincoteague herd, pacing and ambling were more common in the 18th and early 19th century than today, probably because of a higher proportion of Spanish blood in previous centuries. Strong infusions of Arabian and lesser influences of Morgan and Shetland over the last 90-odd years have refined the build of the ponies and decreased the proportion of horses with a natural amble. Mustangs have also been added to the Chincoteague Refuge herd—some of them gaited and carrying Spanish bloodlines, others with lineage tracing to Thoroughbreds, Arabians, and American saddle and draft breeds.

DNA analysis confirms that the Assateague horses have old Spanish heritage. Blood samples taken in the late 1980s revealed shared characteristics with the Paso Fino breed, which descended from animals brought to the New World by the Spanish. The genes of the Assateague herd also closely resemble "cold bloods" such as draft horses and ponies, perhaps a lingering genetic contribution from the Shetland Ponies introduced to promote pinto coloration.

These little horses have long been renowned for their endurance and stamina. Skinner (1843, p. 26) wrote,

> There has been, since long before the American Revolution, on the islands along the sea-board of Maryland and Virginia, a race of very small, compact, hardy horses, usually called beach-horses. . . . They run wild throughout the year, and are never fed. When the snow sometimes covers the ground for a few days in winter, they dig through it in search of food. They are very diminutive, but many of them are of perfect symmetry and extraordinary powers of action and endurance. The Hon. H. A. W[ise]. of Accomac, has been heard to say that he knew one of these beach-horses, which served as pony and hack for the boys of one family, for several generations; and another that could trot his 15 miles within the hour, and was

yet so small that a tall man might straddle him, and with his toes touch the ground on each side [perhaps an exaggeration]. He spoke of another that he believes could have trotted 30 miles in two hours. As an instance of their innate horror of slavery, he mentions the fact of a herd of them once breaking indignantly from a pen into which they had been trapped, for the purpose of being marked and otherwise cruelly mutilated; and rather than submit to their pursuers, they swam off at once into the wide expanse of the ocean, preferring a watery grave, to a life of ignominious celibacy and subjugation!

Legends of Spanish shipwrecks that brought ponies to Assateague Island tend to be vague and produce confusion. John Wallace (1897), for example, acknowledged that the horses had occupied the island "more than a hundred years" (p. 111), "probably two hundred years" (p. 10), or "from time immemorial" (p. 111). Although he conceded that "The traditions relating to their origin are very hazy and improbable," he added, "the most reasonable one, because it is within the range of possibilities, is that a Spanish ship was wrecked off this part of the coast and the original ponies were on board and swam ashore" (p. 111). As late as 1900, locals called Popes Island and Popes Bay Spanish Point and Spanish Bar, claiming that in the 1500s a Spanish galleon wrecked there.

Locals have perpetuated the Spanish legend, though it appears that over 130 years ago, they told a version that featured the wreck of an English vessel. In an 1877 article about Chincoteague in *Scribner's Monthly*, Howard Pyle (p. 737) wrote,

When the first settlers came there, early in the eighteenth century, they found the animals already roaming wild about its piney meadows. The tradition received by the Indians of the main-land was that a vessel loaded with horses, sailing to one of the Elizabethan settlements of Virginia, was wrecked upon the southern point of the island where the horses escaped, while the whites were rescued by the then-friendly Indians and carried to the mainland, whence they found their way to some of the early settlements. The horses, left to themselves upon their new territory, became entirely wild, and probably, through hardships endured, degenerated into a peculiar breed of ponies.

It appears that Pyle confused Chincoteague with Assateague. He was also confused about the "Elizabethan settlements," which were established on and around Roanoke Island, N.C. None of the 16th-century English colonists who left a record reached the Outer Banks from the north or explored the Delmarva Peninsula.

Other dubious stories abound. For example, in a Sunday feature for the *Baltimore Sun*, Donald F. Stewart, director of the Baltimore Maritime Museum, described a Spanish ship, the *San Lorenzo*, wrecked off Assateague in 1820 *en route* to Spain with a cargo that included "3,973 gold doubloons; 173,700 silver pieces of eight; 255 bars of gold; 303 bars of silver; plus a statue of the Madonna and a baptistery, also of solid gold" (Stewart, 1977, p. 17). The shipwreck purportedly carried 95 (or 110) ponies, blinded so they would better accept working in a mine, and released some of them onto Assateague. Langley et al. (2009, p. 72) write, "John Amrhein, Jr. (2007, 187) disputes the authenticity of the existence of this vessel and the associated stories (p. 27) and alleges it was a fiction created by Donald Stewart and believes it is a myth perpetrated through repetition. This needs to be considered seriously as a possibility."

The *San Lorenzo* story has many problems. If the ship had been bound for the mines of Latin America, it might have carried horses, but not treasure, and it would not have passed near Assateague. Spanish ships took horses to the New World in the early days of exploration and settlement, but by the early to mid-1500s Spain was breeding large numbers of fine horses in the Caribbean and on the mainland, enough to support the conquest of two continents.

Moreover, Spain did not have any miniature pony breeds to send to its colonies. Sponenberg states that several breeds in the jaca serrana group of Spanish horses were used for pit ponies, and may have influenced several of the British breeds over centuries, beginning with Roman times. The Shetland Pony, a native of Scotland, was the preferred breed for "pit ponies," and most of these worked the British mines. Pit ponies were almost exclusively stallions and geldings. "The usage is due solely to the fact that you cannot, in such a limited space as a coal mine, have mares and stallions working alongside one another without trouble and loss of work" (Nova Scotia, House of Assembly, 1892). Once employed in a mine, the ponies usually spent their entire lives there. Chronic lung disease often shortened their

Even pregnant, Scotty ET, a 2002 pinto mare, shows beautiful Arabian features. She foaled a few days after the author took this photograph at the April 2011 roundup. Jean Bonde, who donated the mare to the fire company as breeding stock, settled on the name ET because, to her, the marking on her neck resembled the finger of the Hollywood extraterrestrial.

lives and those of their human handlers. Pit ponies were not blinded, but a persistent myth holds that working underground causes them to eventually lose their sight.

Although ships bound *to* Spain from South American mines could have carried treasure, they would not have carried a cargo of maimed miniature horses back to Spain, and the trade routes would not have taken ships bound for Europe anywhere near Assateague. A wreck in the early 1800s would not have provided the foundation stock for the Assateague herd; free-roaming horses had been there for well over a century by then. Any horse restrained in the hold of a ship would have been unlikely to survive a shipwreck. Blind horses would have had virtually no chance at all, though Stewart insisted with apparent seriousness, "blind animals have a greater sense of direction than animals with normal vision" (1977, p. 17). Thompson Holmes and other 19th-century observers who wrote extensively about local livestock did not mention the presence of blind horses on Assateague.

Finally, Dayna Aldridge of Historic Ships in Baltimore (formerly the Baltimore Maritime Museum) admitted no knowledge of the *San Lorenzo* and explained, "our collections . . . are limited to information related to the four ships and lighthouse in our care, thus it is extremely unlikely that we would have any information" (personal communication, January 25, 2012).

At the time of the supposed wreck of the *San Lorenzo*, horses grazed not only on Assateague, but also on many of the other barrier islands of the Eastern Shore; and they ran wild throughout Delmarva and on the mainland. Although it is possible that at least some horses did arrive on Assateague by way of shipwreck(s), just about all of the livestock grazing on necks and islands along the Atlantic coast was apparently placed there by stockmen, and Assateague is probably no different.

Whether these legends are true or not, ships often succumbed to offshore sandbars, bad weather, illusory inlets, and other hazards. Wrecks kept the U.S. Lifesaving Service, established in the 1870s, busy for decades. From the colonial period through the 1960s, at least 156 ships wrecked within the boundaries of Assateague NS. Another 100 or more, including Spanish ships, may have met their fate there or nearby; and wind and currents may have moved parts of offshore wrecks onshore. Blackbeard and other pirates are believed to have sailed the waters surrounding Assateague and used the island's secluded bays and uncharted inlets as hideouts from the Royal Navy and colonial law enforcement .

Coins from many nations have been found along the beach at the north end of Assateague, including 18th- and 19th-century Spanish silver pieces. Spanish treasure ships or pirate vessels that preyed on them may have run aground and spilled their riches on or near Assateague, but Spanish coins found on the dunes do not necessarily denote even a brief Spanish presence. The British Empire prohibited its colonists from minting their own money, so they often used Spanish coins acquired directly, through illegal trade with Latin America, and indirectly from nearly everywhere else. Spanish dollars (pieces of eight) and other currency were accepted around the world and virtually inescapable. After the Revolutionary War, the newly independent United States based its coinage not on the British pound, but on the Spanish dollar. The first silver dollars that it minted in 1794 were the

same size and weight as the latter, and pieces of eight remained legal tender in this country until 1857.

Spanish coins found on Assateague may have come from wrecked Spanish treasure ships, but such vessels riding the westerlies and the Gulf Stream to Spain rarely strayed so far north. Pirates may have stashed the coins, but professional buccaneers were unlikely to hide their loot on a changeable, featureless barrier island. It seems more likely that these coins came from the more mundane wreckage of merchant ships.

The decaying bones of numerous ships have been identified over the years, but new finds keep surfacing. In 2004, an archaeological study found four previously unidentified shipwrecks within the boundary of the national seashore, including the remains of the USS *Despatch*, a 174-ft/53-m wooden-hull steamer that served as the first presidential yacht. Presidents Hayes, Garfield, Cleveland, and Benjamin Harrison used it before it sank in a storm on October 10, 1891. It is probably eligible for the National Register of Historic Places.

Islanders profited from the salvage of shipwrecks, which the residents of Maryland's barrier islands regarded as gifts from the sea or from God. They collected food, furniture, and other items from the wrecks and kept, bartered, or sold them. Many made a very good living from the numerous wrecks, and villages became efficient at dismantling ships that the ocean had sent to them. This became a serious headache for officials in both Maryland and Virginia, who had difficulty enforcing the law on remote Assateague.

In 1799, the Maryland General Assembly appointed a wreck master to control shipwreck sites. He was authorized to command local constables and captains of vessels in the area to cooperate or be fined. Anyone caught plundering a wrecked ship could be sentenced to death. Soon wreck looting was under control and no longer a desirable way for an islander to earn a living, but opportunities for legitimate salvage remained.

From 1522, Spain provided armed escorts for its treasure ships to protect them from pirates and discourage mutineers. Nearly every year from 1566 through 1790, two fortified convoys left Seville (later Cadiz) for New World ports. The *flota* sailed in spring for the Antilles and Mexico; the *galeones*, in summer for South America and Panama. The fleets met at Havana the following year, headed up the Eastern Seaboard to the approximate latitude of Bermuda or the Carolina capes, then steered northeast to take advantage of the Gulf Stream and the westerlies. By the late 1500s some convoys had 100 or more vessels.

Armed escorts protected treasure fleets from hostile vessels, but they remained vulnerable to navigational hazards and bad weather. Storms sank the whole fleet in 1622 and 1715 and caused major losses in 1554 and 1733.

In 1750, a hurricane devastated seven Spanish treasure ships that sailed recklessly into British colonial waters, still hostile despite the formal end of decades of conflict. These ships carried a variety of treasure and goods, as well as a number of distinguished travelers, including the president of Santo Domingo, the viceroy of Mexico, and the governor of Havana. The cargos are well documented and included European prisoners, sugar, medicinal plants, cotton, vanilla, cacao, tobacco, indigo and other dyes, seedlings, hides, gold, silver, mahogany, copper, and large sums of money, for example, about 400,000 pieces of eight whose silver content alone is worth $10 million or more today.

La Galga (Greyhound) probably ran aground on Assateague. Most on board survived, but looters and the churning sea took much of the cargo. *Los Godos*, evidently the only ship carrying livestock, limped into Chesapeake Bay with *San Pedro*, and most of their remaining occupants and cargo found alternate passage to Spain. *Nuestra Señora de Guadalupe* reached Ocracoke, N.C., and set off events that may have inspired Robert Louis Stevenson's *Treasure Island*. The other ships wrecked on the Outer Banks or disappeared.

In 1998, a commercial salvage company, Sea Hunt, located two Spanish wrecks believed to be *La Galga* and *Juno* (1802) and recovered more than 100 artifacts, including coins, anchors, and timber. Spain claimed that it had never abandoned these wrecks and after a legal battle won ownership of both. The Spanish government later allowed the Park Service to exhibit some artifacts at Assateague Island NS.

Amrhein writes in *The Hidden Galleon* (2007) that he believes one of these wrecks was misidentified, and the true remains of *La Galga* rest in Chincoteague NWR. Amrhein asserts that *La Galga, en route* to Spain laden with horses and other valuables, ran aground in a small inlet, long since closed and forgotten. He believes that he has found its remains in what is now an Assateague marsh, and he has appealed to the federal government to have the wreck recognized as a national historic site. The refuge now displays a scale model of *La Galga* in its visitor center. Was *La Galga* one of the wrecks found by the salvage company, or does it lie unexcavated in a marsh? And do the Assateague horses descend from its equine cargo?

We may never know for certain whether the first horses on Assateague arrived by way of shipwreck, but they almost certainly did not originate with the wreck of *La Galga*. First, by all indications, *La Galga* was not carrying horses. Colonists used Assateague for grazing horses and other livestock from the late 1600s. If *La Galga* were really carrying undocumented horses back to Spain—which would have been highly unusual—and if these horses managed to swim to shore when *La Galga* wrecked, they would have found numerous other horses already on the island. Amrhein disagrees, and proposes that the earlier livestock was destroyed by a violent hurricane in 1749 that swept Assateague Island.

Escaping from such a ship would have been difficult. Spanish galleons were large and very sturdy. They were made for warfare and carried formidable armament. Horses in European ships were secured in solid compartments deep within the ship, typically 3 ft x 7 ft/0.9 m x 2.1 m, able to withstand the struggles of a panicked horse and the impact of its body in rough seas. Horses were tethered with ropes short enough to prevent entanglement in stalls too small to allow turning around or backing up. Often their front legs were tied together.

Slings were at times secured around the chest with a breastplate to prevent the animal from falling forward in the stall and breeching across the hindquarters to keep him from falling backwards. When the sea was fair, these hammocks allowed a horse to rest his feet, as the stall was too small to allow him to lie down.

Baron Robert Baden-Powell, the founder of Scouting, was a young captain in the British cavalry when he advised (1885, p. 78),

> The hammock should be slung under the horse's belly loosely, not so tight as to raise him. The breast band and breeching should be securely fastened but not tightly. The object of the sling hammock is to enable the horse to rest himself without actually lying down; but this should only be permitted in fine, calm weather. When the ship is rolling, the hammock should hang quite loose below the horse, so that he will not throw his weight into it, because if he did so he would swing about with every motion of the ship, and so get bruised and chafed. The object of leaving the hammock under him at all in bad weather is to save him falling to the ground if his legs slip from under him; for this reason the fastenings of the suspending ropes of the hammock should be very secure.
>
> In bad weather ashes should be spread over the flooring of the stall to save the horse from slipping. If a horse falls he is very apt to trip up the horse in the next stall with his legs, and one may pass this on to another till a whole number are down.
>
> Should a horse fall, planks, which should always be placed in readiness when bad weather begins, should be run in along both sides of his stall to box him in, and prevent his legs from getting into the next stall.
>
> The men should stand by their horses' heads in rough weather, as the horses will not then be so frightened.

Although some shipwrecks were disasters involving injuries, drownings, and loss of cargo, others were no more than minor strandings. The Lifesaving Service responded to 383 vessels in distress on the Eastern Shore between 1875 and 1915, of which only 174 became total losses. Horses have value, and it would be reasonable to think that owners made an effort to recapture any that escaped to the wild. When damage was minimal, horse-carrying ships were probably evacuated and unloaded with great difficulty, whereupon arrangements

On a gusty November day, the ocean smashes irritably into the Assateague beach. Waves this size could drown swimming ponies, yet they are minuscule compared to the surf of a violent storm.

Although it is possible for horses to swim to shore from a shipwreck in a stormy sea, the odds are not in their favor. Horses swim with their heads low in the water, and high waves are likely to drown them.

were made for another mode of transportation. Any equine castaways joining the wild herd would have most likely been strays that eluded recapture or those who had outlived their shipmates, their owners, or their usefulness.

Escaping from the carcass of a shattered ship and swimming to shore through monstrous storm-driven waves would have been an extraordinary feat for an unaided horse. It would be akin to a horse freeing himself from a narrow horse trailer overturned in a lake, except that the shipwrecked animal was below decks and restrained not only by a halter, head tie, and hobbles, but also perhaps by breastplate, breeching, and sling. The ship was typically afloat, aground, or sinking not in still water, but in violent waves.

Horses would be most likely to survive shipwrecks if someone freed them. On smaller ships, horses stayed on deck, legs hobbled together in fair weather. During storms, their bodies were tied down securely, but left uncovered and exposed no matter how harsh the weather (*History of Race Riding*, 1999). Horses on deck could be more easily released by passengers or crew, and perhaps were more likely to survive than their counterparts belowdecks.

Major shipwrecks typically occurred in storms. If horses got free of a stricken ship, they needed to reach shore to survive, and drowning was a strong possibility. Horses swim with their chins in or near the water, nostrils narrowed to slits just above the surface; high waves can easily overwhelm them. If they made it to shore, the violence of the surf could smash them on the beach with a force sufficient to break long, slender legs. Ponies standing on dry land sometimes drown when storm surge engulfs Assateague in a strong nor'easter or a hurricane.

In the hurricane of 1821 known as the "Great September Gust" the ocean pulled back, exposing bare sandbars, then leapt forward in a giant wave that engulfed both Assateague and Chincoteague "and in an unbroken mass swept across the low south marsh flats, carrying away men and ponies like insects; rushing up the island, tearing its way through the stricken pine woods" (Pyle, 1877, p. 743). A wire story about the Chesapeake-Potomac Hurricane of August 1933 reported that hundreds of ponies drowned and only three survived ("Chesapeake Storm Killed Hundreds of Wild Ponies," 1933, p. 6). Maryland Conservation Commissioner Swepson Earle predicted that Pony Penning might never recover. The 1933 reports were evidently exaggerated—Pony Penning seems to have occurred the next summer without incident (DeVincent-Hayes & Bennett, 2000, p. 104)—but all these accounts underscore the susceptibility of horses to drowning.

In the Ash Wednesday Storm of 1962, roughly half of the Assateague herd was swept into the sea and drowned—about 20 bodies later washed up (Ryden, 2005)—while almost 100 ponies drowned on Chincoteague (Mariner, 2003). A minor storm with high waves swallowed 12 horses on the Maryland end of Assateague in 1992. Sometimes

The Assateague Lighthouse still casts its light over an especially danger-
ous part of the Atlantic coast.

horses disappear in storms and their bodies are never recovered; the
assumption is that they were swept away and drowned.

To minimize the dangers of the Assateague coastline, the first
lighthouse to stand guard over these waters became operational
in 1833. By 1852, officials decided that this structure was neither
tall enough nor bright enough. The present lighthouse, atop a
22-foot/6.7m hill on the Virginia end of Assateague, has been in service since 1867. The 142-foot/43.3-m structure was an unadorned
brick column similar in appearance to the Currituck Beach Light in
North Carolina until the 1960s, when it was painted with distinctive red and white stripes (U.S. Fish and Wildlife Service, 1999). In
2004, the U.S. Coast Guard transferred ownership of the Assateague
Island Lighthouse to the Fish and Wildlife service, which opened it
to the public for climbing.

Lanman (1856) wrote that there were only four families living on
Assateague, those of the lightkeeper and three fishermen. Homes were
constructed ruggedly to withstand the wrath of storms. Assateague
islanders of the 1800s grew produce in gardens fenced to keep the
ponies, sheep, and other animals out. They harvested the trees for
firewood and building materials, collected wool from free-roaming

sheep, and raised hogs in pens. White-tailed deer and huge flocks of migrating waterfowl provided game.

Eventually small, short-lived settlements appeared on Assateague. The villagers were mostly families of watermen, stockmen and, after 1875, employees of the U.S. Lifesaving Service. Assateague Village was the largest of these settlements, and at its peak it contained just over 200 people. In the 1920s factories were built in Assateague Village to process fish into fertilizer and oil. Evaporated seawater yielded salt.

Assateague Village was largely self-sustaining. Former resident Bill Jester (1977, p. 12) recalled in an interview,

> We didn't get many supplies. . . . They could kill all the fowl they wanted to eat. . . .
>
> They had their own hogs, all they had to do was turn 'em loose and get one. And if they wanted beef they had cattle the same way that ran loose on the beaches.

Assateague Village petitioned the state to fund a school, but 40 students had to be enrolled. Assateague residents satisfied this requirement in 1890 by enrolling children as young as age 3. In 1919, a small church was added to the community—before this, religious services were held in the schoolhouse.

For centuries, free-roaming livestock of Chincoteague and Assateague were regularly corralled and branded to determine ownership, a practice that became known as Pony Penning (Wallace, 1897). In all probability, the practice began in the late 1600s or early 1700s. Pony and cattle penning has been practiced on Assateague since before records were kept, and sheep penning is said to have predated them.

Said Refuge Inn founder Donald Leonard (2006, pp. 5–6) in an oral history interview,

> Sheep was as much as a part of the livestock history as ponies or cattle was. . . .
>
> It was a lot a cattle on Assateague before Fish and Wildlife bought it. In fact, there were far more cattle than there was ponies. . . .
>
> And, of course, the beach goes from here to Ocean City. And it was a large area and supported a lot a cattle and horses. But when Fish and Wildlife bought it, of course, they forced the removal of all livestock except the ponies. And the fire

company negotiated a grazing right from Fish and Wildlife, which stands today.

Assateague's sheep penning festivities took place in June, after the annual oyster harvest drew to a close. An 1891 article in a mainland newspaper reported, "The sheep penning at Assateague . . . was attended by some 500 or 600 people, the largest gathering ever known on a similar occasion" ("Chincoteague," 1891, p. 3). As the turn of the century approached, visitors could ride a steamship from the mainland to Chincoteague and back the following day for a dollar a head ("Local News," 1898). The final sheep penning was conducted in 1914. Thereafter, only ponies were gathered.

Up to 75 horses were owned by a single individual, and many people owned just one or two (Mariner, 2003). Pony Penning originated as a necessary chore, but over time it became formalized and ritualized, a cause for festivities (Mariner, 2003). There was one main annual summer penning, as there is today, and smaller pennings at other times of the year (Schoenherr, 2010).

An 1874 newspaper article reported,

> At present the island is said to contain about five hundred of those diminutive horses, who travel in herds and bear the brands of various owners. Some thirty persons live on the island and claim to own all this wild stock in lots or herds of from ten to 100 head. ("Wild Horses in Maryland," 1874, p. 3)

Pony penning was apparently a long-standing tradition on Assateague when the practice was regularly adopted on Chincoteague (Mariner, 2003). Two Chincoteaguers kept large herds of ponies on Wildcat and Piney Island marshes and in the mid-1800s began to pen them annually near the intersection of today's Beebe Road and Ridge Road. At one point, the stockmen attempted to capture the horses without the use of pens, allowing them to escape. When horses were killed in the process, the practice was abandoned in favor of penning. Holmes wrote, "The catastrophe . . . did occur on Chincoteague island, of horses rushing into the sound, when indiscreetly attempted to be caught without pens, by driving detached portions of them upon narrow, projecting marshes; and some fine creatures were drowned" (1835, p. 419). (These drownings in shallow interior waters in controlled circumstances underscore how difficult it would be for horses to swim ashore from a wreck in a stormy sea.)

Holmes (1835, pp. 418–419) commented at length on the history and economics of pony penning:

> The horses of Assateague Island belonged principally to a company, most of whom resided upon the peninsula. No other care of them was required, than to brand and castrate the colts, and dispose of the marketable horses, all of which was effected at the period of their annual pennings (June), the whole, nearly, being joint stock. . . .
>
> The wild gang of Assateague horses were secured by driving them into pens, made for the purpose, of pine logs. The horses seized in the pens, (by islanders accustomed to such adventures, who pushed fearlessly into the midst of the crowded herd,) were brought to the main land in scows, and immediately backed, and broke to use; their wild, and apparently indomitable spirit deserting them after being haltered and once thrown, and subdued by man. More docile and tractable creatures could not be found.

Every summer, Chincoteaguers and men from all over would participate in the capture, branding, and sale of the Assateague ponies, and this occasion developed into a major event that drew crowds and spawned parties. Originally, the roundup involved the entire length of Assateague, then a peninsula, from Ocean City, Maryland, to Toms Cove, rather than gathering them from fenced sections of the Chincoteague refuge as is done today. Holmes (1835, pp. 417–418) described his experience with penning in the early 1800s:

> The multitudes of both sexes that formerly attended these occasions of festal mirth, were astonishing. The adjoining islands were literally emptied of their simple and frolic-loving inhabitants, and the peninsula itself contributed to swell the crowd, for fifty miles above and below the point of meeting. All the beauty and fashion of a certain order of the female population, who had funds, or favorites to command a passage, were sure to be there. . . . It was a frantic carnival, without its debauchery. The young of both sexes, had their imaginations inflamed by the poetical narratives of their mothers and maiden aunts . . . the mad flight of wild horses careering away along a narrow, naked, level sand-beach at the top of their speed, with manes and tails waving in the wind before a company of

mounted men, upon the fleetest steeds, shouting and hallowing in the wildest notes of triumph, and forcing the affrighted animals into the angular pen of pine logs, prepared to enclose them: and then the deafening peals of loud hurras from the thousand half-frenzied spectators, crowding into a solid mass around the enclosure, to behold the beautiful wild horse, in all his native vigor, subdued by man, panting in the toils, and furious with heat, rage and fright; or hear the clamorous triumphs of the adventurous riders, each of whom had performed more than one miracle of equestrian skill on that day of glorious daring—and the less discordant neighing of colts that had lost their mothers, and mothers that had lost their colts in the *melee* of the sweeping drive, with the maddened snorts and the whinnying of the whole gang—all, all together formed a scene of unrivaled noise, uproar and excitement, which few could imagine who had not witnessed it, and none can adequately describe.

But the play of spirits ended not here. The booths were soon filled, and loads of substantial provision were opened, and fish and water fowl, secured for the occasion, were fried and barbacued by hundreds, for appetites whetted to marvellous keenness by early rising, a scanty breakfast, exercise and sea air. The runlets of water and the jugs of more exhilerating liquor, were lightened of their burden. Then softer joys succeeded: and music and the dance, and love and courtship, held their undisputed empire until deep in the night.

It seems that little has changed in the past 200 years.

An 1874 newspaper article ("Wild Horses in Maryland," p. 3) offered a similar perspective:

On Chincoteague Island, the square in front of the Atlantic Hotel is used for a pen, but on Assateague a large pen has been built on the shore of stout pine logs. Men and boys mount tame ponies and start out to bring in the herds. They gallop to pasture grounds, and, after much yelling, fast riding, and some little swearing, they manage to drive one of the herds down to the shore. Nearly all the houses on Chincoteague are built along the sound, and the yards in front join each other, thus forming a continuous fence. When the herds get started down the shore the riders press close after, yelling and whooping, and there is a lively chase until the avenue that leads to the pen is reached. Here a crowd of men are standing, and they turn the head of the flying column into the square. Some of the ponies suspect treachery and run into the water, but the riders dash after them, and soon the whole herd is forced into the pen. The colts stick close to their dams and in all the rearing and plunging about through the pen they never become separated.

On the eve of the Civil War, Charles Lanman interviewed 82-year-old Rev. David Watts, then said to be the oldest resident of Horntown, Virginia, on the mainland near Chincoteague. Lanman wrote (1856, pp. 235–236),

By far the most interesting circumstance connected with the wild horses of Assateague had reference to the annual festival of penning the animals for the purpose of, not only of bringing them under subjection, but of selling them to any who might desire to purchase. The day in question was the 10th of June, on which occasion there was always an immense concourse of people assembled on the island from all parts of the surrounding country; not only men, but women and children; planters who came to make money, strangers who wished to purchase a beautiful animal for a present, together with grooms or horse-tamers, who were noted at the time for their wonderful feats of horsemanship.

But a large proportion of the multitude came together for the purpose of having a regular frolic, and feasting and dancing were carried on to a great extent, and that too upon the open sandy shore of the ocean, the people being exposed during the day to the scorching sunshine, and the scene being enlivened at night by immense bonfires, made of wrecked vessels or drift wood, and the light of the moon and the stars. The staple business of these anniversaries, however, was to tame and brand the horses, which were usually cornered in a pen, perhaps a hundred at a time, when, in the presence of the immense concourse of people, the tamers would rush into the midst of the herd, and not only noose and halter the wild and untamed creatures, but, mounting

Pony pennings in the 19th century were action-packed events in which cowboys wrangled defiant ponies in a rousing East Coast rodeo. "Crossing to Assateague," by Howard Pyle (1877, p. 743), courtesy of Cornell University Library, Making of America Digital Collection.

them, at times, even without a bridle, would rush from the pen and perform a thousand fantastic and daring feats upon the sand.

Few, if any, of these horsemen were ever killed or wounded while performing these exploits, though it is said that they frequently came in such close contact with the horses as to be compelled to wrestle with them, as man with man. But, what was still more remarkable, these men were never known to fail in completely subduing the horses they attempted to tame; and it was often the case that an animal which was wild as a hawk in the morning could be safely ridden by a child at the sunset hour.

Pyle (1877, p. 741) describes the process of capturing a single pony in the corral:

The momentous time arrives for casting the lasso; not as they do in the West, but by hanging it on the end of a long pole, and then dropping it skillfully over the pony's head. Uncle Ken takes the pole. Holding the noose well aloft on the top of it, so as not to frighten the intended prey upon which he has fixed his eye, he cautiously approaches the herd, around which the crowd has gathered. One of the ponies takes a sudden fright and a stampede follows, the spectators scattering right and left. For a moment the intended captive is wedged in the midst of the rest of the herd. Uncle Ken sees his advantage. He rushes forward, the noose is dropped and settles around the pony's neck. Immediately six lusty negroes, with glistening teeth, perspiring faces and glittering eyes, are at the other end of the rope. The animal makes a gallant fight. This way and that he hauls his assailants, rearing and squealing. Now he makes a sudden side dash and sends them rolling over and over, plowing their heads through the shifting sand till their wool is fairly powdered; still, however, "the boys" hold on to the rope. At length the choking halter commences to tell; the pony, with rolling eyes and quivering flanks, wheezes audibly. Now is the moment! In rush the negroes, clutching the animal by legs and tail. A wrestle and a heave, a struggle on the pony's part, a kick that sends Ned hopping with a barked shin like a crazy turkey, and Sambo plowing through the sand and stinkweed in among the spectators, and then over goes the pony with four or five lusty shouting negroes sprawling around him. The work is done: a running noose is slipped around the pony's nose, his forelock is tied to this by a bit of string, and soon his tantrums cease as he realizes that he is indeed a captive.

These cowboys were often black men, many of them freed slaves. By the 1880s, pennings were held on Chincoteague one day and Assateague the next in addition to the traditional Assateague sheep penning.

Scott's Ocean House was a privately owned hotel and resort from about 1869 to 1894. It operated at Green Run Inlet on Assateague just north of the state line. The inlet closed in 1880. The hotel was immensely popular, and it attracted an affluent clientele who feasted on local seafood, visited the beach, and enjoyed the ballroom and bowling alley. Nearby Ocean City attracted mostly local people while Scott's drew visitors from as far away as Pennsylvania and West Virginia. In time, Ocean City added homes, hotels, cottages, and boarding houses and blossomed into a fashionable resort area with a boardwalk that workers disassembled and stored during the off season.

After tying her legs with rope and laying her flat, Chincoteague volunteer firemen trim the hooves of a feisty filly who is in no mood for a pedicure. Photograph circa 1940s, from the collection of Flickr user rich701.

Waterfowl are abundant on Assateague, but not nearly as numerous as they were before the arrival of Europeans. Through the 19th century, on Assateague and elsewhere, egrets, geese, and other birds were hunted relentlessly even during the breeding season and at night. The seemingly unreducible avian population dropped precipitously through the 1800s.

One author observed of Chesapeake Bay in 1830,

The quantity of fowl of late years, has been decidedly less than in times gone by; and the writer has met with persons who have assured him, the number has decreased one half in the last fifteen years. This change has arisen, most probably, from the vast increase in the destruction from the greater number of persons who now make a business or pleasure of this sport; as well as the constant disturbance they meet with on many of their feeding grounds, which induces them to distribute themselves more widely, and forsake their usual haunts. (Sharpless, 1830, p. 41)

Where once birds arose from the waters in amorphous clouds to be felled in great numbers by the most inept gunner, flocks shrank and individual species became endangered. Waterfowl and other birds were hunted commercially for meat and for feathers (which adorned women's hats) and for sport until the Migratory Bird Treaty Act of 1918 (16 U.S.C. §§ 703–712) limited the harvest to ducks, geese, and other game birds. It also gave the federal government the power to establish seasons for game birds and set other limits.

Hunters congregated in camps, cabins, and lodges and shot from blinds, watercraft, and the shore. Gunning shantyboats—shallow-draft, flat-bottom houseboats—were commonplace in Mid-Atlantic marshes from the 1880s to the early 1900s. Hunters could retreat to the marshes and shoot waterfowl for up to a week at a time.

In Virginia, where land on Assateague was unavailable to gun clubs, sportsmen found a loophole that allowed them access to the wild flocks. Clever hunters leased oyster beds, which granted them the right to build oyster watch houses, structures used by oystermen to monitor oyster grounds. When legislation prohibited the construction of new oyster houses, sportsmen placed trailer homes on oyster scows—floating watch houses that became readily available as the oyster industry declined. These scows were eventually prohibited because they lacked sewage holding tanks.

Another reason for the decline in waterfowl was the widespread practice of collecting wild bird eggs for food and as a social activity. "Egging" was popular on Assateague as early as the 18th century. Communities planned picnics for the purpose of harvesting delicacies from the nests of marsh and seabirds. Assateague "eggers" primarily foraged on two rookery islands in Sinepuxent Bay, Great Egging Beach, and Little Egging Beach, near the old ferry landing on the Maryland portion, but also visited Green Run Beach, just north of the state line, and North Beach, at the north end of the island.

Chincoteague was home to a number of year-'round residents. By 1835, the Island of Chincoteague supported in excess of 70 families, a number that more than doubled by 1860. In 1881 John Bunting built a fish factory on Chincoteague where Atlantic menhaden (*Brevoortia tyrannus*), small inedible fish, were converted to oil, which was used in cosmetics, paints, and lamps. The dried fish pulp was sold as fertilizer. Chincoteague residents grew potatoes, strawberries, and corn, but mostly made their living from the sea. The island was renowned for the distinctively flavored oysters that grew there in great quantities. Access to the mainland railroad increased local watermen's income by allowing them to supply New York and Philadelphia with oysters, trout, and channel bass.

Pyle wrote in 1877 (p. 738),

> There are two distinct classes of inhabitants upon Chincoteague: the pony-owners—lords of the land—and the fishermen. Your pony-owner is a tough, bulbous, rough fellow, with a sponge-like capacity for absorbing liquor; bad or good, whisky, gin, or brandy, so that it have the titillating alcoholic twang, it is much the same to him. Coarse, heavy army shoes, a tattered felt hat, or a broad-brimmed straw that looks as if it had never been new; rough homespun or linen trowsers, innocent of soap and water, and patched with as many colors as Joseph's coat; a blue or checked shirt, open at the throat, and disclosing a hairy chest,—these complete his costume. Your fisherman, now, though his costume is nearly similar, with the exception of shoes (which he does not wear), is in appearance quite different. A lank body, shoulders round as the bowl of a spoon, far up which clamber his tightly strapped trowsers; a thin crane-like neck, poking out at right angles from somewhere immediately between the shoulder-blades; and, finally, a leathery, expressionless, peaked face, and wiry hair and beard complete his presentment.

When Virginia communities took sides at the onset of the Civil War, Chincoteague voted almost unanimously to remain with the Union—mainly because islanders sold their seafood to northern markets. The Union, however, seldom acknowledged their fidelity, and it seized Chincoteague ships and cargo in northern ports.

As the natural bounty dwindled, watermen took to planting oyster beds as they would other crops. Starting around 1864, watermen selected "seed" oysters from the "rocks"—public beds—and distributed them in their private beds, growing them in shallow water for 12–18 months, then deeper water for the next year or so. The beds were then allowed to lie fallow for a year, and the process began again. Chincoteaguers leased the oyster beds from the state for 50 cents a year, and eventually much of the area surrounding Chincoteague Island was used for oyster farming. The flavor of the oysters was influenced by whether they were grown on mud, shell, or sand, and they were popularly deemed good for eating only during months with an *r* in their names, or September through April.

The industry boomed. During the 1879–1880 season, 318,113 bushels of oysters (roughly 11,200 m³ or 8,000 tons/7,300 metric tons) were harvested from the waters surrounding Chincoteague and exported by ship or rail (Mariner, 2003). In 1890, this number rose to 300–400 bushels a day. Chincoteague oystermen set the all-time record in 1889, sending out 1,600 bushels by rail in a single day. In 1913 alone, Chincoteague shipped 60,000 barrels/7,000 m³ of in-shell oysters and 80,000 gallons/303,000 L of shucked oysters.

In the 1930s, the newly constructed Ocean City Inlet jetty system increased the salinity of the estuaries adjoining Assateague and increased the numbers of native oyster predators, such as starfish. Chincoteague oysters were overharvested, eelgrass (*Zostera marina*) was struck by a virus and all but disappeared, and in the 1950s two aggressive single-celled oyster parasites, MSX (*Haplosporidium nelsoni*) and dermo (*Perkinsus marinus*), infected oyster beds. These multiple insults sent the oyster population into sharp decline until the Chincoteague oyster was in danger of disappearing altogether (Hayward, 2007). Atlantic bay scallops (*Aequipecten irradians concentricus*) were also affected by these events, though with the resurgence of eelgrass, they have begun a modest comeback.

During the 1920s one man, Dr. Samuel Field of Baltimore, owned much of the south end of Assateague and denied others in the community access to the shellfish beds of Toms Cove. At that time about 25 families lived on Assateague, most in Assateague Village, facing Chincoteague near the lighthouse, where they maintained a school, a church, and two stores. Field employed a guard from

Although many oyster watch houses were erected to monitor oyster beds or to allow hunters access to waterfowl, this house on Tom's Cove was built as a recreational property. In recent years it has grown unstable, and the primary residents are a nesting pair of ospreys that raised chicks in a nest built over the chimney.

Wyoming, Cooper H. "Cowboy" Oliphant, in 1921. Cherrix (2011, p. 74) says that Oliphant was hired "to be the manager of his stock farm and to collect rents from the people leasing the flats and oyster grounds. He was known to dress like a cowboy, ride a big horse, and carry a big gun." Finally, the frustrated residents floated their homes across the channel on barges and set up residence on Chincoteague.

Field owned the land, but not all the free-roaming horses on Assateague. Annual penning, sorting, and branding events had determined ownership every year, probably from the late 1600s. The centuries-old ritual came to an abrupt end in 1921 because Field would not let the stockmen cross his land to gather the horses. In 1922, the locals established a single penning on Chincoteague for both islands. Initially, ponies were ferried across from Assateague by boat, but soon stockmen began the tradition of swimming them across the channel, as is done today.

Around the turn of the 20th century, Chincoteague had become prosperous and had its own schools and hotels, a post office (established in 1854), and many homes. The island was home to two separate communities, "Up the Island" and "Down the Island," each with a church, a school, and general stores. Up the Island, or "Oysterville," even had a separate post office for a short time. These villages gave rise to several neighborhoods—Deep Hole, Downtown, Down the Marsh, Up the Neck, Snotty/Rattlesnake Ridge, and Chicken City (Hall, Reed, & Daisey, 2012; Waterhouse, 2003)—with subtle differences in speech and sometimes-testy relations: "They'd run you out . . . if you tried to court a girl from one of these different neighborhoods. They'd chunk you with rotten eggs and brickbats and everything!" (Hall et al., 2012, p. 13).

Warren (1913, pp. 776–777) wrote of her experience with the Chincoteague people on a visit 15 years earlier:

> The people marry early, the girls sometimes at the age of fourteen, the men at eighteen, and they have large families. One woman is pointed to as the mother of eighteen children; another was a grandmother at thirty. . . . These people are encompassed by the poetry of life—by the three most ancient cries in the world: the cry of the sea-bird, the call of the wind, and the sighing of the sea. Yet they live according to a happy prose kept resolutely in their blood by the strong Anglo-Saxon strain in them, which has come down as unchanged perhaps as in any community in the world. And allowing for surface changes, they live much as their fathers did. . . . There was no mayor and no prison, and, after the first rage, people forgave easily whatever crime was committed.

When Warren returned in 1913, the town was considerably more modern, with gas lamps, telephones, and two five-cent theaters. A chambermaid told Warren, "Things hain't like they were when you came before. We have a bathroom now; you can lie right down in the tub and let the water go all over you" (Warren, 1913, p. 777).

Livestock still ranged freely on the island, and herds of cattle and hogs regularly wandered into town. Mariner (2003) recounts that Clark Street was once called Madcalf Lane. It was so named after a boy walking his girlfriend home in the dark stumbled over what he thought was a log, which turned out to be a sleeping calf. The heifer leaped up and ran off with the boy on her back.

After reading about the island in national publications, visitors flocked to the town. In the late 1800s, a steamboat named *Chincoteague* carried passengers and freight between the mainland at Franklin City, Va., and the island. Chincoteague was incorporated as a town in 1908.

Free-roaming animals were outlawed on Chincoteague in the early 20th century, and any wandering stock was impounded—at the same address as the municipal jail! In the spring of 1920, workers began constructing a causeway linking Chincoteague to the mainland, a project completed in 1922. On the opening day, amid fanfare and parades, a rainstorm turned the causeway into a quagmire, stranding 96 cars in the dark.

The streets were narrow, and the wooden houses were close together. The people of Chincoteague feared fire because they knew that it could quickly wipe out much of their community. Their fears became reality in the early 1900s when a fire did considerable damage (Chincoteague Volunteer Fire Company, n.d.). Residents bought a hand-pump fire engine, then later a gasoline engine, and trained a team to use it. But when a serious fire struck on September 5, 1920, the equipment had fallen into disrepair and would not work properly. Twelve homes and businesses were lost, including the hotel, the post office, the shoe-repair shop, and the bank. As it turned out, the fire was set by 15-year old Etman Cherrix, who had been offered $10 to perform the deed by a resident trying to commit insurance fraud (Mariner, 2003).

The resilient town quickly recovered and rebuilt itself. Four years later, another fire took most of the buildings on the west side. Chincoteague residents vowed that this preventable tragedy would never recur. In 1924, residents formed the Chincoteague Volunteer Fire Company. To raise money for equipment, the fire company bought 80 of the ponies running free on Assateague.

Donald Leonard explained,

> I started [participating in] the roundups—I guess in the late 30's, penning not only on Assateague, but on Wallop's Beach. . . . (2006, p. 1)
>
> The ponies were owned by Mr. Joseph Pruitt [of Greenbackville, Va.]. He was a very successful business man and he owned the livestock grazing rights on Assateague and at

that time on Wallops Beach. At his death it became a problem for the fire company in that if the ponies went elsewhere were bought by someone else, the fire company went out of business. . . .

[T]hey were forced to buy as many of the ponies of Joseph Pruitt at the settling of his estate. And that's what put the fire company in the pony business. (2006, p. 5)

The fire company held its first Pony Penning in 1925. Residents organized the annual Firemen's Carnival, which included the roundup and auction of the ponies. Every year, most of the new foals went to the highest bidders, and the adult ponies returned to Assateague to live as wild. Thus the tradition of selling horses to raise money began.

The development of wetlands and the black market for waterfowl and their meat and feathers were putting pressure on many native species. Chincoteague NWR was established in 1943 as a breeding and wintering area for migratory and resident waterfowl. The refuge protected 9,000 acres/3,642 ha of coastal wetlands and wildlife. The land in question, however had been free-range grazing land for hundreds of years, and locals petitioned the U.S. Fish and Wildlife Service to continue this generations-old practice.

In 1943, with the formation of the refuge, the Service issued a permit to Wyle Maddox, allowing him to graze cattle and horses on part of the island. Three years later, the Service issued a special use permit, which allowed the fire company to graze up to 150 horses; since the early 1950s the fire company has owned all the horses on the refuge (Grey, 2014).

Rachel Carson, world-renowned marine biologist, environmentalist, and editor-in-chief for the Fish and Wildlife Service, wrote that when the refuge was created, the agency permitted residents of Chincoteague to graze 300 head of horses and cattle on the refuge, and noted no adverse effect on waterfowl. (Only 150 horses are permitted today.) "The presence of these grazing animals is not detrimental to the waterfowl for which the refuge was established," she said (1947, p. 17).

Later, the Fish and Wildlife Service removed the cattle and opposed the ponies as a nuisance that trampled vegetation and competed with the birds for forage. The refuge erected fences to restrict their range to

Although the Fish and Wildlife Service worked to eradicate the ponies from the Chincoteague National Wildlife Refuge, Pony Penning continued on schedule, as shown in this photograph from the 1940s. From the collection of Flickr user rich701.

only 5% of the Virginia section of Assateague (Ryden, 2005). Almost all of this section was salt marsh, which provides plenty of food, but offers no way to escape the torment of insects and no high ground to climb in storms.

When the Ash Wednesday Storm of 1962 flooded the Assateague lowlands, about half the horses in the refuge drowned (as did nearly 100 horses on Chincoteague). In 1965, the fences were reconfigured to give the ponies access to high ground and to let them range more freely (Ryden, 2005).

On Chincoteague, the storm wrought great damage as well. In *Stormy, Misty's Foal* (1963), Marguerite Henry gives a fictional account that nonetheless accurately captures the horrors of the aftermath. Grandpa Beebe had died some years before the storm; but in Henry's story, he, Paul, and waterman Tom Reed combed the flooded pastures in the Deep Hole section of Chincoteague in a scow to flag the bodies of drowned ponies so that crews could remove them by helicopter. First the boat bumped into the body of Black Warrior, one of Grandpa's favorite stallions, then swirling crows led them to the bodies of Warrior's mares and foals. Grandpa surveyed the scene dejectedly. Henry wrote (1963/2007, 119–120),

> It was almost as if they were alive. Some were half-standing in the water, propped up by debris. . . .
>
> Then he took a good look, and he began to name them all, saying a little piece of praise over each. . . .
>
> "That Black Warrior was a good stallion. He died tryin' to move his family to safety, but . . . " his voice broke " . . . they just couldn't move."
>
> The heart-breaking work went on. . . . They found more stallions dead, with their mares and colts nearby. And they found lone stragglers caught and tethered fast by twining vines. As the morning dragged into noon, and noon into cold afternoon, the pile of flags in the boat dwindled.

The storm surge swamped houses, ripped boats out of their moorings and hurled them through the stores on Main Street, and disinterred bodies. In one cataclysmic event, the once-thriving Chincoteague poultry industry was destroyed, never to recover. Water stood 6 ft/1.83 m deep in spots, and raging fires broke out. Dead fish, chickens, and livestock decomposed by the thousands in the soggy ruins, presenting a health hazard that necessitated the evacuation of the island.

Betts Devine, who grew up on Chincoteague, recalls,

> I spent my summers in my Grandfather's house on Peterson Street on Chincoteague, and I will always remember the five high tide marks on the wall paper in "the big kitchen." Not to mention the way the floor boards were warped in one corner, so the rocking chair was always in a reclined position. . . .
> The two highest marks were from 1938 hurricane and the Ash Wednesday Storm. (Personal communication, April 6, 2012)

Drowning still occasionally claims equine lives. A freak storm with high waves drowned 12 Assateague horses on the Maryland end in 1992. Wildlife biologist Jay Kirkpatrick wrote, "something that can only be described as a small tidal wave" swept across the island, engulfing the animals (1994, p. 141). The storm waters were powerful enough to wash them across the bay and deposit their bodies on the mainland. Some bodies were even found caught in trees.

A Chincoteague mare named Mystery wades through a shallow impoundment, keeping her body protectively between her newborn and the author. Nobody seems to know where she came from—she just appeared in the north refuge herd one day—and she did not come from the Maryland herd.

Besides the danger of storms, wild island ponies are vulnerable to potentially fatal diseases spread by bloodthirsty insects. Eastern equine encephalitis, a neurological disease transmitted from birds by mosquitoes, is responsible for a significant number of pony deaths on Assateague. The virus can also be fatal to humans. In 1960, 30-odd Chincoteague Ponies succumbed to EEE in a span of 10 days. Most of them were foals that "had been held past the regular 'pony-penning' sale and were used in the filming, during July and August, of the motion picture, 'Misty'" (Byrne, 1968, pp. 357–358). The foal that portrayed young Misty herself was the first to contract the disease. Forty more horses in the Maryland herd died from EEE in 1989–1990 (Kirkpatrick, 1994). Another 40 died on Cumberland Island, Georgia, in 1990 (Goodloe, Warren, Osborne, & Hall, 2000). Those years saw an uncharacteristically large mosquito population. The fire company now vaccinates against EEE, but vaccinating the other free-roaming herds would involve stressful and expensive annual gathers—and on heavily forested Cumberland Island, it would be virtually impossible to gather every horse.

The salt marsh is an ideal breeding ground for several species of mosquito, but marshes are not necessary to ensure a large population of the insects. Mosquitoes can successfully breed larvae in water that collects in a broken bottle or a fallen leaf. The dried eggs can survive for up to five years, and a moistening rainfall is enough to trigger their growth. They can hibernate as eggs, larvae, or adults to survive any season, including severe winters. Drawn by the heat, moisture, carbon dioxide, and other chemicals released by warm-blooded species, mosquitoes are most active at dawn and dusk.

In addition to the usual behaviors such as tail-swishing, stomping, head-shaking, and mutual grooming, ponies often wade out into the bay or even the ocean to escape the onslaught of insects. Sometimes they wade out so far that only their heads can be seen. More typically, they move into water deep enough to discourage flies, but shallow enough to let foals nurse—sometimes as much as a half-mile (0.8 km) from shore.

Ponies are familiar with high spots where the wind blows more strongly and often congregate there when the insects are relentless. They plunge into deep brush and rub against trees to dislodge the pests. Horses also have a "fly-shaker" muscle over the shoulder area that can be twitched to remove insects.

In 1974, a colt sold to a family from New Jersey tested positive for equine infectious anemia (swamp fever), a fly-borne chronic equine disease. In 1975, almost half the Chincoteague NWR herd tested positive. The horses in question did not show signs of serious illness and were not likely to die from the disease, at least not in the short term, but state law mandated the quarantine or destruction of positive testers. For three years affected individuals were quarantined on the island, away from other horses, producing disease-free foals that were sold at auction. In 1978, the positive testers were euthanized to halt the spread of the disease.

Officials from the Maryland Department of Agriculture and the Park Service considered testing the Maryland herd for EIA and euthanizing positive reactors, but it would have been an enormous task to corral and test every individual—and very stressful to the horses. If the agencies missed just one horse that carried the disease, the whole herd could be reinfected. To implement such a plan, officials would have had to shoot any animals that evaded capture in order to ensure that the disease was not spread.

The Park Service finally concluded that the drawbacks outweighed the benefits and opted to let the herd remain untested. Because these animals are not sold to mainlanders like the Virginia ponies, the presence or absence of EIA poses no risk to other horse populations. Fences prevent the intermingling of herds. In theory, flies can carry the disease from Maryland ponies to Virginia ponies; but so far, there have been no problems, since horses must be in close proximity to transmit the disease.

In August 1978, a Maryland stallion with EIA crossed the fence at the state line and joined the Virginia herd (Mackintosh, 1982/2003). Over time, other potential carriers circumvented the fence, and, Park Service biologist John Karish laid plans to gather and test all Maryland ponies. The plans were never implemented, and there remains a small risk that Virginia ponies may someday contract EIA from a Maryland horse. The Park Service opens the beach to equestrians only after the fly season, so domestic horses would be unlikely to contract EIA from the wild herd.

Virginia, like most states, prevents the spread of EIA by requiring a Coggins test (antibody screen) of any horse attending an exhibition or sale or transported across state lines. Any horse that contracts EIA must be either quarantined for life or euthanized. In accordance with the law, Chincoteague Ponies must have a negative Coggins test before sale at the annual pony auction.

Epizootics are among the natural pressures that shape a free-roaming herd, and sometimes the medical and scientific communities are powerless to prevent them. Over the years, large numbers of ponies and horses of various breeds have been experimentally infected with equine infectious anemia in laboratories all over the world in hope of developing a vaccine against the dreaded lentivirus. This greatly anticipated vaccine, however, remains elusive.

For decades, professional and student zoologists, botanists, ecologists, oceanographers, geologists, and others have found Assateague ideal for original research (Frydenborg, 2012). Most of their work has increased understanding of the island or its wildlife without harming either. But in the 1950s and 1960s government-sponsored scientists experimented on Chincoteague Ponies from the Virginia herd with different agendas in mind.

For example, at least six teams of researchers studied equine and human influenza by infecting roughly 40–60 ponies and observing the results. The role of these experiments in evaluating influenza as a biological weapon (Wheelis, Rózsa, & Dando, 2006) is unclear, but they were underwritten by institutions that conducted bioweapons research, notably the U.S. Army. The following is a summary:

- Cameron et al. (1967) took 24 yearlings to the University of Maryland in College Park and infected them all with influenza H3N8, a virulent subtype that caused major outbreaks among horses in the United States in 1964–1965. The organism was also apparently responsible for the pandemics of 1889–1890 (Valleron et al., 2010) and 1898–1900 (Salmon, n.d.), and the economically devastating North American equine panzootic of 1872 (Morens & Taubenberger, 2010; Threlkeld, 2010). All infected ponies mounted an immune response. About half grew very ill, with fevers up to 105.2°F/40.7°C (normal is 99–101°F/37.2–38.3°C), respiratory rates as high as 80–90 per minute (normal is 12–24), and a dry cough. All survived, though three were treated for colic.
- Alford, Kasel, Lehrich, and Knight (1967) tested H3N8 on 33 prisoners and on four ponies used in Cameron et al. (1967).
- About a year later, Cameron, Kasel, and Couch (1974) gave eight ponies used in Cameron et al. (1967) an inactivated-virus influenza vaccine and checked their antibodies.
- Kasel, Byrne, Harvey, and Schillinger (1968) infected 12 Chincoteague Ponies of both sexes, all about 18–24 months old, with human influenza, apparently in College Park. It is not clear whether these ponies were veterans of earlier studies.
- Kasel, Fulk, Haase, and Huber (1968) infected an unknown number of Chincoteague Ponies with human influenza A and B in College Park.
- In late 1968, during a pandemic of Hong Kong influenza that killed about 34,000 people in this country and 700,000 worldwide (U.S. Dept. of Veterans Affairs, 2013), Kasel, Fulk,

and Harvey (1969; see also Spaulding, 1968) infected 10 Chincoteague Ponies about 8 months old with the Hong Kong virus and five with A2/Rockville/65, then all 15 with equine influenza (H3N8). Around the same time, Couch, Douglas, Kasel, Riggs, and Knight (1969) infected 15 prisoners with equine influenza (H3N8). Then Couch, Fulk, Douglas, Kasel, and Knight (unpublished, cited in Kasel & Couch, 1969) gave those prisoners the Hong Kong virus. A Hong Kong influenza vaccine existed before this cluster of studies began (Health England, n.d.), so their purpose is unclear.

From 1957 or earlier till 1969 or later, these researchers and others in their network infected burros, domestic horses, and ponies of unknown origin with many other viruses, several of which had been or would be weaponized (Buescher et al., 1963; Byrne, 1963; Bailey et al., 1979; Cameron et al., 1967). Robert J. Byrne of the University of Maryland mentions "Stored, frozen brains of horses and ponies from which EEE virus has been isolated over the past 6 years" (Byrne, 1963, p. 6), but says nothing about the ponies' breed, manner of infection, or cause of death. The project received support from the Army Medical Research and Development Command at Fort Detrick, Md., which took interest in the bioweapon potential of these viruses.

Army-affiliated researchers also conducted research on or near Assateague in the 1960s. One team tested birds, mosquitoes, and 156 ponies from Chincoteague, Assateague, and the mainland for Eastern equine encephalitis (Byrne, 1963). There was even a small facility supported by several agencies on Assateague itself. What occurred at the Assateague Research Laboratory is unclear, though the Fish and Wildlife Service (USFWS, 1962, p. 22) described it as an "improvised temporary laboratory for study of encephalitis at Chincoteague Wildlife Refuge." It moved to Wallops Island by mid-1963.

The Army was well past its horse-drawn era when it became really interested in communicable diseases of horses and other livestock. When the United States entered World War II, Germany, Japan, and the Soviet Union already had biological warfare programs (Beck, 2003). In 1942, the civilian War Research Service hastily developed the first American bioweapons at Camp (later Fort) Detrick. Its successor, the Army Chemical Warfare Service, manufactured approximately 5,000 anthrax bombs, but did not deploy them during the war

(Lindler, Lebeda, & Korch, 2005; Ryan, 2008). Other American factories geared up to produce vast quantities of anthrax, brucellosis, tularemia, Q fever, and VEE pathogens. A plant in Vigo, Indiana, could turn out *100 tons of anthrax spores a month* (Ryan, 2008).

After the Third Reich fell, Allied governments quietly recruited, rescued, or captured German scientists and engineers (Boyne, 2007; Hunt, 1991). As a result, American and Soviet BW programs flourished during the Cold War. Researchers refined old bioweapons and developed new ones: bubonic plague, rabies, *Staphylococcus* (bacterial pneumonia, food poisoning, toxic shock syndrome, and flesh-eating infections), *Clostridium botulinum* (botulism), and several deadly hemorrhagic fever viruses (Ebola, Marburg, Lassa, and Rift Valley) (Beck, 2003; Greif & Merz, 2007). Some of this research helped develop vaccines, antisera, and therapeutic agents to protect troops and noncombatants from biological attack (Laird, 1970; Smith et al., 1997; Wheelis, Rózsa, & Dando, 2006), but its focus was offensive.

To investigate the real-world performance of bioweapons, the U.S. Army ran 239 or more clandestine tests of biological agents and proxies on American soil from the 1940s through the 1960s (Carlton, 2001). In one 1950 exercise, a Navy ship sprayed bacterial fog for 6 days over the San Francisco Bay area. The main agent, *Serratia marcescens*, was deemed harmless; but it evidently killed a 75-year-old civilian and sent others to the hospital, and it may have had delayed effects, such as a meningitis outbreak in 2001 (Carlton, 2001; Tansey, 2004). The Army tracked dispersal by adding the toxic, carcinogenic fluorescent compound zinc cadmium sulfide.

Army files released during 1977 U.S. Senate hearings document biological and chemical tests on unsuspecting subjects in most of the eastern and central United States and parts of Canada, in Manhattan subways, at Washington National Airport, even inside the Pentagon (Carlton, 2001; Cole, 1997; Mangold & Goldberg, 2000; Rubin, 2007; Subcommittee on Zinc Cadmium Sulfide, 1997; Wheelis, Rózsa, & Dando, 2006). Until information leaked out in the 1970s, the public knew nothing about the open-air tests or laboratory experiments on thousands more military and civilian subjects.

Safety concerns, political pressure, and advances in other weapons eventually made the American biological arsenal dispensable. President Nixon formally abolished this country's offensive BW capability in 1969 (Ryan, 2008; Tucker & Mahan, 2009). Coincidentally or not, experiments on Chincoteague Ponies apparently ended around the same time.

Other countries still possess or have acquired biological weapons, and the menace of bioterrorism is growing. Long after the Chincoteague-related research seemingly ended, several viruses studied remain high on the Army's threat list: "The viral encephalitides represent 15% (9 of 62) of the infectious diseases identified by the Armed Forces Medical Intelligence Center as being of U.S. military operational importance" (Hoke, 2005, p. 92).

Offensive and defensive BW programs seem equally porous. In 1977, a distinctive H1N1 influenza strain that had been extinct in humans more than two decades suddenly appeared in China, which officially labeled the event "mysterious." Western virologists maintained that the only rational explanation for the unchanged reemergence of a rapidly mutating virus is escape from a laboratory freezer. Anthrax caused 100 deaths near Sverdlovsk, USSR, in 1979 (Greif & Merz, 2007). Ft. Detrick was evidently the source of anthrax used in postal attacks that killed five and sickened 17 in 2001 (Meyer, 2008), and three vials of VEE virus that disappeared from there in 2009 are still missing (Shaughnessy, 2009).

In nature, viruses evolve to afflict specific hosts and typically cause benign infections in these reservoir species (Mandl et al., 2011; Seale, 1989). When a virus jumps to a novel host, it is likely to cause severe illness (Mandl et al., 2011). In humans, pathogens that originated in animals often cause pandemics, for example, "HIV (from chimpanzees), SARS coronavirus (from bats) and influenza A virus (from birds)" (Flanagan, Leighton, & Dudley, 2011, p. 2; Sharp, Shaw, & Hahn, 2005). Smallpox and measles evolved from mutations of cowpox and rinderpest, pathogens that affect cattle (Diamond, 2009).

Influenza A continually reshuffles its genetic structure within its natural reservoir of wild birds (Taubenberger & Morens, 2013). Sometimes, in a process incompletely understood, it infects either domestic fowl or mammals, including humans, swine, horses, dogs, cats, and seals. Some virologists worry that introducing viruses into novel hosts in a laboratory encourages them to jump species and turn virulent (Taubenberger & Morens, 2013). Cameron et al. (1967) inoculated ponies with equine influenza virus grown in kidney tissue cultures from rhesus monkeys, green monkeys, and *human embryos*. Other researchers gave human subjects equine influenza. Many of the studies discussed here could have promoted cross-species transmission. One must wonder how they affected public health, how many other wild herds have been living laboratories, and whether any post-World War II disease outbreak among them was natural.

Researchers chose Chincoteague Ponies for influenza experiments because serum samples confirmed that this convenient herd was naive to influenza. Although Assateague is a tourist attraction, they deemed the herd "relatively isolated from humans" with "no known previous contact with other equines" (Cameron et al., 1967, p. 510). Most of the studies explicitly refer to Chincoteague Ponies from Assateague. The 28 horses living on the Maryland end when the Park Service took over in 1968 could not have supplied so many unique subjects. The Virginia herd is the only possible source, but there is no evidence that the refuge or the fire company knowingly provided ponies for experimentation. Nor is there evidence that researchers bid against tourists at the annual auction.

Still, the 15 weanlings studied by Kasel et al. (1969) must have come from the 1968 crop of foals, and the 24 ponies used by Cameron et al. (1967), with ages in a 6-month spread, probably belonged to an earlier cohort. Cameron et al. (1967) acknowledged Thomas J. Reed (1901–1993) of Chincoteague for "advice and assistance in securing the ponies for the experiments" (p. 515), and Kasel et al. (1968, p. 969) thanked him for unspecified "assistance." Reed was a prominent local figure—market gunner, waterfowl breeder, decoy carver, character in Marguerite Henry's *Stormy* (1963), and 24-year contract employee of "John Hopkins/Walter Reed" [*sic*] (Hall et al., 2012, p. 2)—yet his role in procurement is unknown.

Did research on Chincoteague Ponies cause the deadly outbreak of EEE on Chincoteague and Assateague in October 1960? More likely, it was a natural occurrence. EEE is endemic to East Coast barrier islands and follows natural cycles of resurgence and quiescence. The Fish and Wildlife Service (USFWS, 1962) says the Assateague Laboratory was created between July 1, 1960, and December 30, 1961, to study "whether birds are important in transmission of encephalitis to man and horses" (p. 21) and seems to suggest that the 1960 epizootic led to the laboratory, not vice versa:

"The isolated refuge area was ideal for the virus transmission study because of the presence of wild ponies, a large bird population, and the known occurrence of the virus in the area" (p. 22). And though researchers in the Army network did infect ponies with EEE, there is no indication that these ponies were from or on Assateague. Many questions arising from this troubling episode remain unanswered or unasked.

Whenever an epizootic or natural disaster has devastated the Chincoteague refuge herd, the public has responded with donations and support as soon as the news hit the wire. In 1976, the equine infectious anemia crisis on Chincoteague caught the attention of Bob Evans, sausage maker and owner of a thriving restaurant in Ohio that would become a chain worth $1.7 billion. In 1972, Evans had acquired five mustangs with strong Spanish Barb characteristics captured in Utah and New Mexico. He freed them to roam his 1,000-acre/405-ha farm near Rio Grande, Ohio. Evans was distraught when he heard of the crisis on Assateague. "Here is an animal that was almost extinct," he said. "Something has to be done, and done quickly" ("Mustangs to cross breed with endangered pony herd," 1976, p. 14). He donated two young Spanish Barb stallions from his mustang herd to fortify the Chincoteague bloodlines.

Harry Bunting, a seafood dealer and chairman of the Chincoteague Volunteer Fire Company, applauded Evans's donation: "Centuries of inbreeding may have made the ponies more susceptible to disease and Spanish Barb blood should serve to strengthen the wild ponies of Assateague for future generations" ("Mustangs to cross breed with endangered pony herd," 1976, p. 14).

To revitalize the gene pool further and rebuild the population, the fire company imported 38 mostly solid-colored Western mustangs from a U.S. Bureau of Land Management adoption center near the California-Nevada state line in 1977. Bunting chose bays, blacks, and grays to bring the Chincoteague herd back to the solid colors he remembered from childhood. They "really look nice," he said. "I went out West to pick them out myself . . . they're having a problem getting rid of them out there and I thought here was 38 we could save from a can" ("Mustangs Not Accepted, Yet," 1977, p. 6).

According to Bunting, the fire company introduced new stock to the herd every 8 to 10 years, using mustangs, Arabians, and Morgan

Saltwater Cowboys come from great distances to assist in the three annual round-ups of the Chincoteague ponies. Their mounts are invariably taller than their free-roaming counterparts and comprise many breeds.

Chincoteague

horses. "Otherwise you'd have a herd of idiots. They'd interbreed so," he said ("Breeding Horses Come East," 1977, p. 5).

At first the ponies shunned the mustangs, leaving them to form bands of their own. Challenged by the lower nutrient content of the forage and the relentless biting insects, most of these mustangs failed to adapt to the barrier island and died within a year (Keiper, 1985). Tim Ferry, a native of Alexandria, Va., recalls spotting mustangs during family vacations in the 1970s (personal communication, July 6, 2013).

> It was easy and fun to pick the remaining ones out because they were BIG horses, at least most of them. Some would dwarf even the largest Chincoteague pony standing at 14 hands plus. . . .
>
> [A] very special, beautiful wild mustang stallion [was] added to the Chincoteague herd in the 1970's and stayed around into the year 1982. . . . His foals for a few years went the highest at the auction. I believe the first $1,000 foal was his too. He had one of the largest herds on the island.

The fire company had also added mustangs in 1939, when it acquired 20 from Nevada for genetic diversity (Szymanski, 2007). It is unclear how many of these survived.

Over the years, the fire company has introduced other outside horses to the Chincoteague NWR herd to expand the gene pool and to improve quality, but it has not kept complete records of changes to herd composition. In the early 1900s, Shetland Ponies were added to promote pinto coloration, leaving this group with a greater proportion of pony genes that also decreased the average height (Keiper, 1985). A 1925 newspaper article notes, "The strain is not so pure now as it was in former years. The Shetland pony together with other breeds has been introduced, and the effect has wrought variety" ("Pony Round-Up at Chincoteague to Be the 'Wild West' Show of East," 1925, p. 3). Another article says that Samuel Field "improved" roaming horses "by the importation of valuable stallions" (Marinus, 1929). In 1945, when the National Advisory Committee for Aeronautics, the predecessor of NASA, purchased Wallops Island, the free-roaming ponies that inhabited it were gathered and moved to Assateague (DeVincent-Hayes, Bennett, & Hayes, 2001, p. 16).

A tall bay mustang towers over the native ponies as they rest in a pine forest on the south side of Beach Road. Many of the mustangs added to the herd were taller and heavier than the island ponies. Photograph by Tim Ferry, taken in the 1980s.

Well-bred Arabian horses have also been added to the herd. Al-Marah Sunny Jim was a chestnut Arabian stallion donated to the fire company in 1965 ("Al Marah Sunny Jim," 2012). He was bred to Misty's daughter Stormy twice, producing Rainy and Misty II. He was also bred to Assateague mares and may have been released on the island.

Skowreym, a purebred 1953 gray Arabian stallion was leased to the fire company for two years. A grandson of the celebrated Raffles ("Skowreym," 2012), the 14.1-hand (57-in./1.45-m) gray was a seasoned endurance horse who often placed first or second in high-profile 50- and 100-mile (80- and 161-km) rides. On July 25, 1964. Linda Tellington-Jones, internationally acclaimed authority on animal behavior and originator of Tellington TTouch Training®, rode Skowreym (unsuccessfully) on the grueling Tevis Cup Ride— 100 rugged miles/161 km in the Sierra Nevadas. He began his sojourn on Chincoteague shortly thereafter.

Many of the outside horses introduced by the fire company were unable to adapt to the barrier island environment and died within a few years. In the mid-1990s, the fire company sent a group of Assateague mares to renowned trainer Stanley G. White at Grandeur Arabians in Florida to mate with purebred Arabian stallions. One filly and several colts (including the feisty buckskin Copper Moose) were

Surfer Dude, (left), born in 1992, is the direct descendant of Nevada mustangs introduced to the herd in 1978. He was born to a mare with a BLM freeze brand. His sire was reportedly a bay mustang named Pirate, who was later known as "Broken Jaw" after he fractured his mandible in a fight with another stallion.

kept as 1996 buy-backs and have lived long lives infusing the herd with the bloodlines of champions.

Premierre, a 1991 chestnut Arabian stallion with impeccable bloodlines, served mares on Chincoteague, then was released onto Assateague ("Premierre," 2012). He disappeared in 1999. Some believe he was stolen. Some think he died, though no body was recovered. He sired a number of half-Arabian foals, including island patriarch North Star. After Premierre's disappearance, the fire company kept a donated bay Arabian stallion at the carnival grounds with a group of mares. The registration papers of the resulting foals give his name as Striking Gold; but he was registered under a different name, and the Arabian Horse Association Registry and local sources are unsure of his true origins.

Old photographs can shed light on herd composition. An image taken at Pony Penning in 2000 and circulated on the Internet among

A graceful Arabian stallion crosses a marsh in the south pasture of the Chincoteague NWR in 1987. Arabians have been periodically out-crossed into the herd to infuse the resulting foals with exotic beauty, elegance, and stamina. Photograph by Tim Ferry.

Chincoteague Pony enthusiasts depicts an elderly bay mare in the Assateague corral with the south herd. She has a prominent BLM freeze brand on her neck indicating that she was born in 1973 in Nevada. Another image from the 1981 Pony Penning shows an Appaloosa mare and foal, probably mustangs. These two were the only known Appaloosas on Assateague, and it does not appear that this line contributed to the present-day herd.

The 2013 interim Chincoteague Pony management plan signed by Pony Committee Chairman Harry S. Thornton states "A wide variety of breeds such as Morgan, Welsh, Shetland, Arabian, and Mustangs were placed in the Chincoteague pony herd to increase genetic diversity and vigor among the present stock" (Grey, 2014, p. D-17). Other evidence for herd introductions is anecdotal. "Back then, record keeping was not high on their list of priorities, and some of the 'old heads' of the fire company have long since passed away," said Denise Bowden (personal communication, February 5, 2011). Szymanski (2007) writes that Quarter Horses were introduced in the 1960s, and at other times horses and ponies were turned out to run with the herd, details of their heritage lost to time. One former

Eastern Shore resident remembers a 1960s news photograph purportedly portraying a Thoroughbred herd sire named "Red" leading a band of Chincoteague mares.

Betts Devine, who spent her childhood on Chincoteague and is a distant cousin of Maureen Beebe of *Misty* fame, recalled,

> My mother was born in 1921, and she remembers the ponies as being between 12 and 14 hands high (she was horse- and pony-crazy all of her life), and being mostly solid colors—bays, browns, chestnuts, and an occasional black. As she grew older, and western movies showed the "painted Indian ponies," the ponies on Assateague were bred with pinto stallions, to produce "splashy" paints. With the Chincoteague Volunteer Fire Company in charge of the breeding of the ponies, since the herds were decimated by the Ash Wednesday Storm, select mares (those with good conformation) have been bred to select stallions to improve the breed and keep from too much in-breeding. Mares have gone to Quarter horse, Morgan, Paint, and Arabian stallions. (Personal communication, April 6, 2012)

The fire company tried to maintain the vigor of the herd not only by importing Arabians and mustangs, but also by keeping natives. Sometimes the fire company agrees to accept a previously auctioned horse as a donation. Witch Doctor, a striking dark bay pinto, was sold as a foal to a farm in New York. After the young stallion escaped to cohabit with the wrong group of mares, the fire company agreed to take him back to his Assateague birthplace (Szymanski, 2012). Witch Doctor found his place among the island stallions and acquired a respectable harem.

In the past, ponies from the Maryland herd have been transferred to the Virginia part of the island. Over time, the Park Service relocated 44 Maryland horses to the Virginia herd before the start of immunocontraception in 1994 (Zimmerman, Sturm, Ballou, & Traylor-Holzer, 2006). Many of these horses were notorious for causing difficulties with campers by being too bold or by damaging property in their quest for human food. All horses tested negative for EIA before joining the Chincoteague herd.

Other returns are less compatible with island life. A young stallion was released on Assateague in 2008 and proceeded to engage in

After the swim-back event, a flotilla of spectators in kayaks shadows the ponies back to their fenced enclosures on Assateague. Kayaking affords an optimal vantage point for the pony swim if the visitor is willing to paddle the distance to the crossing site.

serious combat with the island stallions. He attacked with the fearlessness of a kamikaze, earning himself the name of Chaos. The Fire Company decided to sell him before the herd sires suffered serious injury, and he found a peaceful new home with a Maryland breeder (Szymanski, 2012).

The bloodlines of the introduced horses have blended with the native island stock to create a unique breed, the Chincoteague Pony. To keep lines pure, the fire company no longer introduces foreign stock into the refuge population. When outside genes would benefit the health of the herd, a genetically suitable foreign mare may be introduced to mate with a stallion and give birth. After weaning, the foal would remain on the refuge to continue the lineage, while the mare would return to the mainland (Grey, 2014).

Each of the ponies has a story worth telling, but some are legendary. The 1995 stallion Miracle Man started life as an orphaned foal found in Black Duck Marsh by carver, tour boat operator, and Chincoteague town councilman Arthur Leonard. Wearing dress clothes and shoes, Leonard waded into the marsh to rescue the newborn, but the foal was too quick. It took a team of volunteers hours to capture him. The foal had been motherless for several days and had abscesses on his eye and leg. The Leonard family coerced a lactating mare into nursing him and tended to his wounds. He wintered in Florida with a friend of the Leonards, who lavished attention on him and taught him how to bow and shake hands. The fire company released him onto Assateague as a yearling, and in time he became a successful and much-admired harem stallion (Szymanski, 2012).

Miracle Man was a smart stallion with an uncanny internal calendar. Just before the 2008 Pony Penning, the clever horse drove his mares into the channel and swam them to Memorial Park on Chincoteague four days ahead of schedule. (The palomino pinto stallion Prince did the same thing with his band in 2012.)

Another noteworthy Leonard performed a dramatic rescue of a black-and-white mare frozen in an Assateague pond, apparently dead. The late Donald Leonard was a lifetime member of the Chincoteague Volunteer Fire Company and former chairman of the Pony Committee. He and a friend extracted the unfortunate pony from the ice and found that she had a weak heartbeat. They rushed her to the fire station and rigged a sling to help her stand as she recovered. Icy, as she was named, survived to deliver a black colt in the firehouse, named "Little Icicle" (Szymanski, 2012).

The Chincoteague herd differs markedly in composition from other feral horse herds because of human interference. The majority of foals are sold to mainland homes a few months after birth. More colts are sold than fillies, and some of the fillies and an occasional colt return to the breeding herd every year. This results in a sex ratio of 4.6 mares for every stallion, nearly double the ratio seen in the herd on the north end of the island.

The mean age of each pony in the Chincoteague herd was greater, too. Sixty percent of the Virginia horses are adults; less than 40% were mature in the Maryland herd before birth control began. The foaling rate is also considerably higher in Virginia.

The health of the horses in the Virginia herd is enhanced by the management practices of the fire company, including treatment of injuries, annual deworming to improve use of the food they ingest, and vaccinations to prevent serious illnesses. High birth rates are advantageous in a population where there is no shortage of buyers for foals. With the pony swim and auction attracting new visitors every year and foal prices steadily climbing, the sales of each new colt or filly will boost the fire company's revenue.

Pony Penning week provides children a unique opportunity to observe the behavior of wild horses and to join in the excitement of a roundup.

On Chincoteague, every Pony Penning is at least as exciting as the one before as spectators pack the tiny island in hope of glimpsing the ponies swimming across the channel at slack tide. The details of the horses' origins have been lost to the passage of time, but one thing is clear—the free-roaming horses of Assateague have been in continual residence on the island for centuries, and with conscientious management they may remain in the centuries to come.

Chincoteague

References

Al Marah Sunny Jim. (2012). *Pedigree Online All Breed Database.* Retrieved from http://www.allbreedpedigree.com/al+marah+sunny+jim

Aldridge, D. (2012, January 25). Personal communication.

Alford, R.H., Kasel, J.A., Lehrich, J.R., & Knight, V. (1967). Human responses to experimental infection with influenza A/Equi-2 virus. *American Journal of Epidemiology, 86*(1), 185–192.

Amrhein, J., Jr. (2007). *The hidden galleon: The true story of a lost Spanish ship and the legendary wild horses of Assateague Island.* Kitty Hawk, NC: New Maritima Press.

Anderson, K. (1995). *Feeding and care of orphaned foals* (NebGuide G95-1237-A). Retrieved from http://digitalcommons.unl.edu/cgi/viewcontent.cgi?article=1233

Anderson, V.D. (2002). Animals into the wilderness: The development of livestock husbandry in the seventeenth-century Chesapeake. *William and Mary Quarterly, 3rd Series, 59*(2), 377–408. Retrieved from http://www.jstor.org/stable/3491742

Assateague Island, nature and science. (2010, November 21). Retrieved from http://www.nps.gov/asis/naturescience/index.htm

Baden-Powell, R.S.S. (1885). *Cavalry instruction. Course of lectures ordered by General Order 30, dated 1st of March, 1884, for instruction of cavalry, yeomanry, & c., & c.* London, United Kingdom: Harrison & Sons.

Beck, V. (2003). Advances in life sciences and bioterrorism. *EMBO Reports, 4* (Special Issue), S53–S56. doi: 10.1038/sj.embor. embor853

Beverley, R. (1705). *The history and present state of Virginia, in four parts.* London, United Kingdom: For R. Parker. Retrieved from http://docsouth.unc.edu/southlit/beverley/beverley.html

Bonde, J. (2010, July 23). Personal communication.

Bonetti, T. (Ed.), (2014) *Chincoteague and Wallops Island National Wildlife Refuges draft comprehensive conservation plan and draft environmental impact statement.* Chincoteague, VA: Chincoteague National Wildlife Refuge.

Boswell, R., & Mason, W. (2010, October 7). *Buyback Babes, island firemen have more to mend than fences.* Retrieved from http://wildponytales.info/archives/1337

Bowden, D. (2011, February 5). Personal communication.

Breeding horses come east. (1977, August 27). *Harrisonburg Daily News-Record* (Harrisonburg, VA), p. 5.

Bruce, P. A. (1907). *Economic history of Virginia in the seventeenth century: An inquiry into the material condition of the people, based upon original and contemporaneous records.* New York, NY: MacMillan.

Buescher, E.L., O'Dell, E.T., Scheider, F.G., Bourke, A.T.C., Eldridge, B.F., Thompson, E.G., . . . Suyamoto, W. (1963). Project 3A 0 12510 A 806: Military preventive medicine. (1963). In *Annual progress report, 1 July 1962–30 June 1963*, Vol. I, pp. 203–220. Washington, DC: Walter Reed Army Institute of Research.

Byrne, R.J. (1968). Sleeping sickness wakes again. In U.S. Department of Agriculture, *Science for better living: The yearbook of agriculture, 1968*, pp. 355–359. Washington, DC: Government Printing Office.

Cahill, A.E., Aiello-Lammens, M.E., Fisher-Reid, M.C., Xia, H., Karanewsky, C.J., Hae, Y.R., . . . Wiens, J.J. (2012, October 17). How does climate change cause extinction? Proceedings of the Royal Society B: Biological Sciences. doi: 10.1098/rspb.2012.1890 1471-2954

Cameron, T.P., Alford, R.H., Kasel, J.A., Harvey, E.W., Byrne, R.J., & Knight, V. (1967). Experimental equine influenza in Chincoteague Ponies. *Proceedings of the Society for Experimental Biology and Medicine, 124*(2), 510–515. doi: 10.3181/00379727-124-31777

Cameron, T.P., Kasel, J.A., & Couch, R.B. (1974). Persistence of antibody to envelope antigens of Heq2Neq2 virus in ponies after infection and vaccination. *Proceedings of the Society for Experimental Biology and Medicine, 146*(3), 658–660. doi: 10.3181/ 00379727-146-38166

Carlton, J. (2001, October 22). Of microbes and mock attacks—Years ago, the military sprayed germs on U.S. cities. *Wall Street Journal.* Retrieved from http://online.wsj.com/news/articles/ SB1003703226697496080

Carson, R. (1947). *Chincoteague: A National Wildlife Refuge* (Conservation in Action 1). Washington, DC: U.S. Fish and Wildlife Service. Retrieved from http://digitalcommons.unl.edu/usfwspubs/1

Cherrix, M.J. (2011). Assateague Island. Charleston, SC: Arcadia Publishing.

Chesapeake storm killed hundreds of wild ponies. (1933, September 5). *New York Times* (New York, NY), p. 9.

Chincoteague. (1891, June 6). *Peninsula Enterprise* (Accomac, VA), p. 3. Retrieved from http://chroniclingamerica.loc.gov/lccn/ sn94060041/1891-06-06/ed-1/seq-3/

Chincoteague Volunteer Fire Company. (n.d.). *Chincoteague Volunteer Fire Company history, 1905–1950.* Retrieved from http://cvfc3. com/about-us/history

Cohen, J. (2011, October 17). *Did Jamestown's settlers drink themselves to death?* Retrieved from http://www.history.com/news/ did-jamestowns-settlers-drink-themselves-to-death

Cole, L.A. (1997). *The eleventh plague: The politics of biological and chemical warfare.* New York, NY: Henry Holt.

Couch, R.B., Douglas, Jr., R.G., Kasel, J.A., Riggs, S. & Knight, V. (1969). Letters to *Nature.* Production of the influenza syndrome in man with equine influenza virus. *Nature, 224*(5218), 512–514. doi: 10.1038/224512a0

Convention on the Prohibition, Development, Production, and Stockpiling of Bacteriological (Biological) and Toxin Weapons and on Their Destruction, April 10, 1972, 26 U.S.T. 583, 1015 U.N.T.S 163, retrieved from http://www.unog.ch/80256EDD006B8954/(httpAssets)/C4048678A93B6934C1257188004848D0/$file/BWC-text-English.pdf

Covington, H.F. (1915). The discovery of Maryland, or Verrazzano's visit to the Eastern Shore. *Maryland Historical Magazine 10*(3), 199–217.

DeVincent-Hayes, N., & Bennett, B. (2000). *Chincoteague and Assateague islands.* Charleston, SC: Arcadia Publishing.

DeVincent-Hayes, N., Bennett, B., & Hayes, J.R. (2001). *Wallops Island.* Charleston, SC: Arcadia Publishing.

Doney, S.C., Ruckelshaus, M., Duffy, J.E., Barry, J.P., Chan, F., English, C.A., . . . Talley, L.D. (2012). *Annual Review of Marine Science, 4,* 11–37. doi: 10.1146/annurev- marine-041911-111611

Dunbar, G.S. (1958). *Historical geography of the North Carolina Outer Banks.* Louisiana State University Studies, Coastal Studies Series 3. Baton Rouge: Louisiana State University Press.

Duncan, P., & D'Herbes, J.M. (1982). The use of domestic herbivores

in the management of wetlands for waterbirds in the Camargue, France. In D.A. Scott (Ed.), *Managing wetlands and their birds: A manual of wetland and waterfowl management. Proceedings of the third Technical Meeting on Western Palearctic Migratory Bird Management* (pp. 51–56). Slimbridge, United Kingdom: International Waterfowl Research Bureau.

Eggleston, E. (1884, January). Husbandry in colony times. *Century Illustrated Monthly Magazine, 27*(3), 431–448.

Emge, P. (2014, September 7). Personal communication.

Eshelman, R.E., & Russell, P.A. (2004, July 21). *Historic context study of waterfowl hunting camps and related properties within Assateague Island National Seashore, Maryland and Virginia.* N.P.: Eshelman and Associates. Retrieved from http://www.nps.gov/asis/parkmgmt/upload/AssateagueHuntingLodgesStudyFinalReport.pdf

Farrer, J. (1649). *A perfect description of Virginia.* London, United Kingdom: For Richard Wodenoth. Retrieved from http://etext.lib.virginia.edu/etcbin/jamestown-browse? id=J1080

Farrer, J., & Farrer, V. (Cartographers). (1667). *A mapp of Virginia discouered to ye Hills, and in it's Latt: From 35 dg: & 1/2 neer Florida, to 41 deg: bounds of new England....* Retrieved from http://memory.loc.gov/gmd/gmd388/g3880/g3880/ct000903.jp2

Flanagan, M., Leighton, T., & Dudley, J. (2011, June). *Anticipating viral species jumps: Bioinformatics and data needs* [Report Number OSRD 2011 020, Contract/MIPR Number 01-03-D-0017]. Ft. Belvoir, VA: Defense Threat Reduction Agency, Office of Strategic Research and Dialogues.

Force, P. (Ed.). (1846). *American archives: Fourth series. Containing a documentary history of the English colonies in North America ...* (Vol. 6). Washington, D.C.: M. St. Clair Clarke and Peter Force.

Fried, K. (2010, July 18). Where the wild ponies swim. *Parade*, 12.

Friedman, S.M. (n.d.). *The inflation calculator.* Retrieved from http://www.westegg.com/inflation/

Frydenborg, K. (2012). . Boston, MA: Houghton Mifflin Harcourt.

Giffin, J.M., & Darling, K. (2007). *Veterinary guide to horse breeding* (Kindle edition). Hoboken, NJ: Howell Book House. (Original work published 1999).

Goodloe, R.B., Warren, R.J., Cothran, E.G., Bratton, S.P., & Trembicki, K.A. (1991). Genetic variation and its management applications in eastern U.S. feral horses. *Journal of Wildlife Management, 55*(3), 412–421.

Goodloe, R.B., Warren, R.J., Osborn, D.A., & Hall, C. (2000). Population characteristics of feral horses on Cumberland Island, Georgia and their management implications. *Journal of Wildlife Management, 64*(1), 114–121. doi: 10.2307/3802980

Graham, J. (2007, August 7). *Geologic resources inventory scoping summary, Cumberland Island National Seashore, Georgia.* Washington, DC: U.S. National Park Service, Geologic Resources Division. Retrieved from http://www.nature.nps.gov/geology/inventory/publications/s_summaries/CUIS_gri_scoping_summary_2009-0807.pdf

Grey, E. (2014, May). 2013 interim Chincoteague Pony management plan. In T. Bonetti (Ed.), *Chincoteague and Wallops Island National Wildlife Refuges draft comprehensive conservation plan and draft environmental impact statement* (pp. D-1–D-54). Chincoteague, VA: Chincoteague National Wildlife Refuge.

Greif, K.F., & Merz, J.F. (2007). *Current controversies in the biological sciences: Case studies of policy challenges from new technologies.* Cambridge, MA: Massachusetts Institute of Technology.

Grimstad, P.R. (2001). Cache Valley virus. In M.W. Service (Ed.), *Encyclopedia of arthropod-transmitted infections of man and domesticated animals* (pp. 101–104). Wallingford, United Kingdom, and New York, NY: CABI Publishing.

Hall, D. (Interviewer), Reed, T., & Daisey, D. (Interviewees). (2012). *Tom Reed and Dave Hall, Chincoteague, VA March 24, 1989* [Interview transcript]. Retrieved from http://digitalmedia.fws.gov/cdm/singleitem/collection/document/id/911/rec/5

Hall, M., Casey, J., & Wells, D. (2004). A brief history of the Maryland coastal bays. In C.E. Wazniak & M.R. Hall (Eds.), *Maryland's coastal bays: Ecosystem health assessment* (DNR-12-1202-0009) (pp. 2-2–2-16). Annapolis, MD: Maryland Department of Natural Resources, Tidewater Ecosystem Assessment.

Harrison, F. (1927). The equine F F Vs: A study of the evidence for the English horses imported into Virginia before the Revolution. *Virginia Magazine of History and Biography, 35*(4), 329–370.

Hayter, E.W. (1963). Livestock-fencing conflicts in rural America. *Agricultural History, 37*(1) 10–20.

Hayward, L. (2007). *State of the parks: Assateague Island National Seashore, a resource assessment.* Washington, DC: National Parks Conservation Association.

Help preserve access to Assateague Island, VA. (n.d.) Retrieved from http://www.chincoteague.com/preserve-access/

Hening, W.W. (1823). *The statutes at large; Being a collection of all the laws of Virginia from the first session of the legislature in the year 1619* (Vols. 1–2). New York, NY: For the author.

Henry, M. (1947). *Misty of Chincoteague.* Chicago, IL: Rand, McNally.

Henry, M. (2007). *Stormy, Misty's foal.* New York, NY: Aladdin Paperbacks (Original work published 1963).

Hinds, L. (2010, May 21). Personal communication.

The history of race riding and the Jockeys Guild. (1999). Paducah, KY: Turner Publishing.

Hoke, Jr., C.H. (2005). History of U.S. military contributions to the study of viral encephalitis. *Military Medicine, 170*(4), 92–105.

Holmes, T. (1835, November). Some account of the wild horses of the sea islands of Virginia and Maryland. *Farmers' Register, 3*(7), 417–419.

Hooks, R.O. (2006). *Pine Ridge Horse Farm's illustrated guide to the wild pony auction at Chincoteague: A world famous attraction* (2nd ed.). Salisbury, MD: Pine Ridge Horse Farm.

Hunt, L. (1991). *Secret Agenda: The United States government, Nazi scientists, and Project Paperclip, 1945 to 1990.* New York, NY: St. Martin's Press.

Jester, W.F. (1977, December 5). Interview by Karen Croner. Retrieved from http://espl-genealogy.org/cohistory/transcripts/JESTER, BILL.pdf

Jones, H. (1865). *The present state of Virginia* (Original work published 1724). New York, NY: For Joseph Sabin.

Kasel, J.A., & Couch, R.B. (1969). Experimental infection in man and horses with influenza A viruses. *Bulletin of the World Health Organization, 41*(3), 447–452.

Kasel, J.A., Byrne, R.J., Harvey, E.W., & Schillinger, R. (1968). Experimental human B influenza virus infection in Chincoteague Ponies. *Nature, 219*(5157), 968–969. doi: 10.1038/219968b0

Kasel, J.A., Fulk, R.V. & Harvey, E.W. (1969). Susceptibility of Chincoteague ponies to antigenically dissimilar strains of human type A2 influenza virus. *Journal of Immunology, 103*(2), 369–371.

Kasel, J.A., Fulk, R.V., Haase, A.T., & Huber, M. (1968). Clinical investigations in viral infections and diseases. PHS-NIH individual project report, July 1, 1967 through June 30, 1968. Serial No. NIAID-14(c). In *Annual report of program activities, National Institutes of Health, 1967–1968: National Institute of Allergy and Infectious Diseases* (pp. 22–25). [Washington, DC: National Institutes of Health.]

Keiper, R. (2011, May 19). Personal communication.

Keiper, R. (1985). *The Assateague ponies*. Atglen, PA: Schiffer Publishing.

Keiper, R., & Houpt, K. (1984). Reproduction in feral horses: An eight-year study. *American Journal of Veterinary Research, 45*(5), 991–995.

Kirkpatrick, J. (1994). *Into the wind: Wild horses of North America*. Minocqua, WI: Northword Press.

Kirkpatrick, J.F., & Turner, A. (2003). Absence of effects from immunocontraception on seasonal birth patterns and foal survival among barrier island wild horses. *Journal of Applied Animal Welfare Science, 6*(4), 301–308.

Kirkpatrick, J.F., & Turner, A. (2007). Immunocontraception and increased longevity in equids. *Zoo Biology, 25*, 237–244. doi: 10.1002/zoo.20109

Kirkpatrick, J.F., & Turner, J.W. (1991). Compensatory reproduction in feral horses. *Journal of Wildlife Management, 5*(4), 649–652.

Kobell, R. (2006, July 28). Where men saddle up and ponies paddle over. *Los Angeles Times*. Retrieved from http://articles.latimes.com/2006/jul/28/nation/na-saltwater28

Laing, W.N. (1959). Cattle in seventeenth-century Virginia. *Virginia Magazine of History and Biography, 67*(2), 143–163.

Laird, M.R. (1970, July 6). *Memorandum for the president: National security decision memoranda 35 and 44*. Retrieved from http://www2.gwu.edu/~nsarchiv/NSAEBB/NSAEBB58/RNCBW22.pdf

Langley, S.B.M., & Jordan, B.A. (2007). *Archeological overview & remote sensing survey for maritime resources in Maryland state waters from the Ocean City Inlet to the Delaware Line, Worcester*

County, Maryland. Crownsville, MD: Maryland State Historic Preservation Office. Retrieved from http://mht.maryland.gov/documents/pdf/ archeology_mmap_oceancity_survey_dnr.pdf

Langley, S.B.M., Van Driessche, P., & Charles, J. (2009). *Archeological overview and assessment of maritime resources in Assateague Island National Seashore, Worcester County, Maryland, & Accomack County, Virginia* (revised ed.). Crownsville, MD: Maryland State Historic Preservation Office. Retrieved from http://mht.maryland.gov/documents/PDF/Archeology_MMAP_AINS_Overview&Assess_optimized.pdf

Lanman, C. (1856). *Adventures in the wilds of the United States and British American provinces*, Vol. 2. Philadelphia: John W. Moore.

Leonard, D. (2006, April 25). Interview by Margo Hunt. Retrieved from http://espl- genealogy.org/cohistory/transcripts/LEONARD DONALD.pdf

Levin, P., Ellis, J., Petrik, R., & Hay, M. (2002). Indirect effects of feral horses on estuarine communities. *Conservation Biology, 16*(5), 1364–1371. doi: 10.1046/j.1523-1739. 2002.01167.x

Lindler, L.E., Lebeda, F.J., & Korch, G. (2005). *Biological weapons defense: Infectious disease and counterbioterrorism*. Totowa, NJ: Humana Press.

Local news. (1898, June 4). *Peninsula Enterprise* (Accomac, VA), p. 3. Retrieved from http://chroniclingamerica.loc.gov/lccn/sn94060041/ 1898-06-04/ed-1/seq-3/

Lucas, Z., Raeside, J.I., & Betteridge, K.J. (1991). Non-invasive assessment of the incidences of pregnancy and pregnancy loss in the feral horses of Sable Island. *Journal of Reproductive Fertility, 44*(Suppl.), 479–488.

Lynghaug, F. (2009). *The official horse breeds standards guide: The complete guide to the standards of all North American equine breed associations*. Minneapolis, MN: Voyageur Press.

Mackintosh, B. (2003, October 27). *Assateague Island National Seashore: An administrative history*. Washington, DC: National Park Service, History Division. (Original work published 1982.) Retrieved from http://www.nps.gov/asis/parkmgmt/upload/asisadminhistory.pdf

Mangold, T., & Goldberg, J. (2000). *Plague wars: A true story of biological warfare*. New York: Macmillan.

Mariner, K. (2003). *Once upon an island: The history of Chincoteague.* New Church, VA: Miona Publications.

Marinus, J. (1929, September 28). A little journey to Assateague. *Peninsula Enterprise* (Accomac, VA). Retrieved from http://eshore.vcdh.virginia.edu/node/1993

Maryland Department of Natural Resources, Resource Planning. (2005, October). *Assateague State Park land unit plan.* Retrieved from http://www.dnr.state.md.us/irc/docs/00011180.pdf

McCue, P.M. [2009]. *Foal heat breeding.* Retrieved from http://csu-cvmbs.colostate.edu/Documents/learnmares3-breed-foal-heat-2009.pdf

Meyer, J., (2008, August 8). Inquiry sought into anthrax probe. *Los Angeles Times.* Retrieved from http://articles.latimes.com/2008/aug/08/nation/na-anthrax8

Michaels, L. (2010, May 22). Personal communication.

Migratory Bird Treaty Act of 1918, 16 U.S.C. §§ 703–712. (2012).

Morens, D.M., & Taubenberger, J.K. (2010). Historical thoughts on influenza viral ecosystems, or behold a pale horse, dead dogs, failing fowl, and sick swine. *Influenza and Other Respiratory Viruses, 4*(6). 327–337. doi: 10.1111/j.1750-2659.2010.00148.x

Move 'em out: Wild ponies herded for annual penning. (1981, July 30). *Annapolis Capital*, p. 4.

Mustangs not accepted, yet. (1977, October 5). *Radford News Journal* (Radford, VA), p. 6.

Mustangs to cross breed with endangered pony herd. (1976, July 22). *Bryan Times* (Bryan, TX), p. 14.

N.C. Office of Conservation, Planning, and Community Affairs. (2010, August 25). *North Carolina ecosystem response to climate change: DENR assessment of effects and adaptation measures* [Draft]. Retrieved from http://www.climatechange.nc.gov/pages/Climate Change/Climate_Change_Ecosystem_Assessment_Summary.pdf

National Audubon Society. (2007). *Barrier island/lagoon system, Northampton andAccomack counties* (Audubon Important Bird Areas). Retrieved from http://web4.audubon.org/bird/iba/virginia/Documents/Barrier Island_Lagoon System.pdf

National Oceanic and Atmospheric Administration, National Climatic Data Center. (2012, August 21). *Global warming: Frequently asked questions.* Retrieved from http://www.ncdc.noaa.gov/cmb-faq/globalwarming.html

National Oceanic and Atmospheric Administration, National Climatic Data Center (2012, September). *State of the climate: Global analysis for August 2012.* Retrieved from http://www.ncdc.noaa.gov/sotc/global/2012/8

National Wildlife Refuge System Administration Act of 1966, 16 USC § 668dd (2000).

Nevada ponies imported. (1977, August 27). *Annapolis Capital*, p. 5.

Nieves, D.P. (2009, August 26). Application of the Sea Level Affecting Marshes Model (SLAMM 5.0.2) in the Lower Delmarva Peninsula (Northampton and Accomack counties, VA / Somerset and Worcester counties, MD). Arlington, VA: National Wildlife Refuge System Conservation Biology Program. Retrieved from http://www.slammview.org/slammview2/reports/LDP_ChincoteagueFinal.pdf

Nova Scotia, House of Assembly. *Journal and Proceedings* (1892) at 119.

Peck, K.J. (2008). *Horse husbandry in colonial Virginia: An analysis of probate inventories in relation to environmental and social changes* (Unpublished honors thesis). College of William and Mary, Williamsburg, VA.

Pendleton, E.A., Williams, S.J., & Thieler, E.R. (2004). *Coastal vulnerability assessment of Assateague Island National Seashore (ASIS) to sea level rise* (U.S. Geological Survey Open-File Report 2004-1020, Electronic Book). Retrieved from http://pubs.usgs.gov/of/2004/1020/images/pdf/asis.pdf

Percy, G. (1625). A trewe relacyon of the p[ro]cedeings and ocurrentes of momente w[hi]ch have hapned in Virginia.... Retrieved from http://www.history.org/foundation/journal/winter07/A Trewe Relation.pdf

Pilkey, O., Rice, T., & Neal, W. (2004). *How to read a North Carolina beach.* Chapel Hill: University of North Carolina Press.

Pippin, J. (2005, January 11). Head 'em up, move 'em out. *Jacksonville Daily News* (Jacksonville, NC). Retrieved from http://www.jdnews.com/news/horses-19054-herd-island.html

Pleasants, B. (1999). *Chincoteague pony tales.* Columbus, GA: Brentwood Christian Press.

Chincoteague

Pony Round-Up at Chincoteague to Be the "Wild West" Show of East. (1925, August 3). *Lawrence Journal-World* (Lawrence, KS), p. 3. Retrieved from http://news.google.com/newspapers?nid=2199 &dat=19250803&id=xNZkAAAAIBAJ&sjid=zHUNAAAAIBAJ &pg=2990,4305946

Premierre. (2012). *Pedigree Online All Breed Database.* Retrieved from http://www. allbreedpedigree.com/premierre

Proposed Comprehensive Conservation Plan (CCP) for the Chincoteague National Wildlife Refuge: Oversight Hearing before the Subcommittee on Fisheries, Wildlife, Oceans and Insular Affairs of the Committee on Natural Resources, U.S. House of Representatives, 112th Cong. 9 (2012a) (testimony of Wendi Weber).

Proposed Comprehensive Conservation Plan (CCP) for the Chincoteague National Wildlife Refuge: Oversight Hearing before the Subcommittee on Fisheries, Wildlife, Oceans and Insular Affairs of the Committee on Natural Resources, U.S. House of Representatives, 112th Cong. 14 (2012b) (testimony of Jack Tarr).

Proposed Comprehensive Conservation Plan (CCP) for the Chincoteague National Wildlife Refuge: Oversight Hearing before the Subcommittee on Fisheries, Wildlife, Oceans and Insular Affairs of the Committee on Natural Resources, U.S. House of Representatives, 112th Cong. 17 (2012c) (testimony of Wanda Thornton).

Protocol for the Prohibition of the Use of Asphyxiating, Poisonous or other Gases, and of Bacteriological Methods of Warfare, June 17, 1925, 26 U.S.T. 571, 94 L.N.T.S. 65, retrieved from http://disarmament.un.org/treaties/t/1925/text

Public Health England. (n.d.). *Influenza pandemics—history.* Retrieved from http://www.hpa.org.uk/Topics/InfectiousDiseases/ Infections AZ/PandemicInfluenza/History/

Pyle, H. (1877, April). Chincoteague, the island of Ponies. *Scribner's Monthly, 13*(6), 737–746.

Rennicke, J. (2007, Fall). A climate of change. *National Parks, 81*(4), 26–31.

Rood, R.N. (1967). *Hundred acre welcome: The story of a Chincoteague pony.* Brattleboro, VT: Stephen Greene Press.

Rubin, J. (2007). *The living weapon: Program transcript.* Retrieved from http://www-tc.pbs.org/wgbh/americanexperience/media/ uploads/special_features/download_files/weapon_transcript.pdf

Rudman, R., & Keiper, R.R. (1991). The body condition of feral ponies on Assateague Island. *Equine Veterinary Journal, 23*(6), 453–456. doi: 10.1111/j.2042-3306.1991.tb03760.x

Ryan, C.P. (2008). Zoonoses likely to be used in bioterrorism. *Public Health Reports, 123*(3), 276–281.

Sallenger, A.H., Jr., Doran, K.S., & Howd, P.A. (2012). Hotspot of accelerated sea-level rise on the Atlantic coast of North America. *Nature Climate Change, 2*, 884–888. doi: 10.1038/nclimate1597

Salmon, R. (n.d.). *Swine flu: What next?* National Public Health Service for Wales, Communicable Disease Surveillance Centre. Retrieved from http://www.wales.nhs.uk/sites3/Documents/882/R Salmon.pdf

Schoenherr, I. (2010, September 12). *"That miserable engagement"* [Web log post]. Retrieved from http://howardpyle.blogspot. com/2010/09/that-miserable-engagement.html

Seale, J. (1989). Crossing the species barrier—Viruses and the origins of AIDS in perspective. *Journal of the Royal Society of Medicine, 82*(9), 519–523.

Sharp, G.B., Kawaoka, Y., Jones, D.J., Bean, W.J., Pryor, S.P., Hinshaw, V., & Webster, R.G. (1997). Coinfection of wild ducks by influenza A viruses: Distribution patterns and biological significance. *Journal of Virology, 71*(8), 6128–6135.

Sharpless, J.T. (1830). Chesapeake duck shooting. *Cabinet of Natural History and American Sports, 1*, 41–46. Retrieved from http://www.scribd.com/doc/85925483/The-Cabinet-of-Natural-History-and-American-Rural-Sports-Vol-1

Shaughnessy, L. (2009, April 22). *Army: 3 vials of virus samples missing from Maryland facility.* Retrieved from http://edition.cnn. com/2009/US/04/22/missing.virus. sample/index.html

Shomette, D.G. (2008). The price of amity: Of wrecking, piracy, and the tragic loss of the 1750 Spanish treasure fleet. *The Northern Mariner/le marin du nord, 18*(3–4), 25–48.

Skinner, J.S. (1843). The horse, in England and America—As he has been, and as he is. In W. Youatt & J.S. Skinner, *The horse* (2nd ed.) (pp. 17–34). Philadelphia, PA: Lea and Blanchard.

Skowreym. (2012). *Pedigree Online All Breed Database.* Retrieved from http://www. allbreedpedigree.com/skowreym

Smith, J. (1624). *The generall historie of Virginia, New-England, and the Summer Isles.* London, United Kingdom: For Michael Sparkes.

Spain loans artifacts to Assateague Island National Seashore. (2007, September 12). Retrieved from http://www.nps.gov/history/archeology/sites/npsites/assateague.htm

Spaulding, J. (1968, December 21). Flu virus may first grow potent in animals. *Milwaukee Journal*, p. 19.

Spies, J.R. (1977). *The wild ponies of Chincoteague*. Cambridge, MD: Tidewater Publications.

Sponenberg, P. (2014, June 5). Personal communication.

Stewart, D.F. (July 24, 1977). Assateague ponies: A new look at their origin. *Baltimore Sun*, pp. 14–17.

Subcommittee on Zinc Cadmium Sulfide, Committee on Toxicology, Board on Environmental Studies and Toxicology, Commission on Life Sciences, National Research Council. (1997). *Toxicologic assessment of the army's zinc cadmium sulfide dispersion tests*. Washington, DC: National Academy Press.

Szymanski, L. (2007). *Out of the sea: Today's Chincoteague pony*. Centreville, MD: Tidewater Publishers.

Szymanski, L (with Emge, P.). (2012). Chincoteague ponies: Untold tails. Atglen, PA: Schiffer Books.

Taggart, J.B. (2008). Management of feral horses at the North Carolina Estuarine Research Reserve. *Natural Areas Journal, 28*(2), 187–195.

Tansey, B. (2004, October 31). Serratia has dark history in region/ Army test in 1950 may have changed microbial ecology. *SFGate*. Retrieved from http://www.sfgate.com/health/article/Serratia-has-dark-history-in-region-Army-test-2677623.php

Tateo, A., Maggiolino, A., Padalino, B., & Centoducati, P. (2013). Behavior of artificially suckled foals. *Journal of Veterinary Behavior, 8*(3), 162–169.

Taubenberger, J.K., & Morens, D.M. (2013). Influenza viruses: Breaking all the rules. *mBio, 4*(4). doi: 10.1128/mBio.00365-13

Terry, R. (2010, July 27). Personal communication.

Threlkeld, L. (2010, January 24). The Great Epizootic: Sick horses bring the economy to a square halt. *Eventing Nation*. Retrieved from http://eventingnation.com/home/the-great-epizootic-sick-horses-bring-the-economy-to-a-square-halt.html

Todd, J.D., Lief, F.S., & Cohen D. (1970). Experimental infection of ponies with the Hong Kong variant of human influenza virus. *American Journal of Epidemiology, 92*(5), 330–336.

Town of Chincoteague. (2010). *Beach access questionnaire*. Retrieved from http://www.chincoteague.com/preserve-access/Survey-Summary.pdf

Tucker, J.B., & Mahan, E.R. (2009, October). *President Nixon's decision to renounce the U.S. offensive biological weapons program* [Center for the Study of Weapons of Mass Destruction Case Study 1]. Washington, DC: National Defense University Press.

Turner, A. (2011, February 17). Personal communication.

U.S. Department of Veterans Affairs. (2013, May 30). *Pandemic influenza (flu)*. Retrieved from http://www.pandemicflu.va.gov/about/index.asp

U.S. Environmental Protection Agency. (2013, January 8). *Future climate change*. Retrieved from http://epa.gov/climatechange/science/future.html

U.S. Fish and Wildlife Service. (1999, December). *Assateague Island Lighthouse*. [Washington, DC]: Author.

U.S. Fish and Wildlife Service. (2012, August). *Chincoteague National Wildlife Refuge Comprehensive Conservation Planning Newsletter*. Retrieved from http://www.chincoteague.com/pdfs/usfws_newsletter_aug_2012.pdf

U.S. Fish and Wildlife Service, Bureau of Sport Fisheries and Wildlife. (1962, June). *Wildlife research progress* [Bureau of Sport Fisheries and Wildlife, Circular 146]. Washington, DC: U.S. Fish and Wildlife Service, Bureau of Sport Fisheries and Wildlife.

Upshur, T.T. (1901). Eastern-Shore history. *Virginia Magazine of History and Biography, 9*(1), 88–99.

Vallandigham, E.L. (1893, August 27). An island of ponies: American rivals of the little Shetlands. *Boston Sunday Globe*, p. 28.

Valleron, A.-J., Cori, A., Valtat, S., Meurisse, S., Carrat, F., & Boëlle, P.-Y. (2010). Transmissibility and geographic spread of the 1889 influenza pandemic. *Proceedings of the National Academy of Sciences of the United States of America, 107*(19), 8778–8781). doi: 10.1073/pnas.1000886107

Vavra, M. (2005). Livestock grazing and wildlife: Developing compatibilities. *Rangeland Ecology & Management, 58*(2), 128–134. doi: 10.2111/1551-5028(2005)58<128:LGAWDC>2.0.CO;2

Virginia Commission on Boundary Lines. (1873). *Report and accompanying documents of the Virginia commissioners appointed to ascertain the boundary line between Maryland and Virginia*. Richmond, VA: R.F. Walker, Superintendent of Public Printing.

Wallace, J.H. (1897). *The horse of America in his derivation, history, and development.* New York, NY: Author.

Warren, M.R. (1913, October). The island of Chincoteague. *Harper's Monthly Magazine, 127*(761), 775–785.

Washburn, R.M. (1877). *The peoples' condensed library: A compendium of universal knowledge.* Chicago, IL: Author.

Waterhouse, E. (2003). *Chincoteague summer of 1948: A waterman's childhood stories.* Lincoln, NE: iUniverse.

Wheelis, M., Rózsa, L., & Dando, M. (2006). *Deadly cultures: Biological weapons since 1945.* Cambridge, MA: Harvard University Press.

Wild horses in Maryland. (1874, February 19). *Indiana Progress* (Indiana, PA), p. 3.

The wild ponies of a Virginia island. (1910, July 21). *Arizona Republican* (Phoenix), p. 9.

Willis, D. (1995, July 25). Humane Society protests pony penning and sale. *Baltimore Sun* (Baltimore, MD). Retrieved from http://articles.baltimoresun.com/1995-07-25/news/1995206053_1_pony-humane-society-sale

Wise, J.C. (1911). *Ye Kingdome of Accawmacke or the Eastern Shore of Virginia in the seventeenth century.* Richmond, VA: Bell Book and Stationery.

Zimmerman, C., Sturm, M., Ballou, J., & Traylor-Holzer, K. (Eds.). (2006). *Horses of Assateague Island population and habitat viability assessment workshop: Final report.* Apple Valley, MN: IUCN/SSC Conservation Breeding Specialist Group.

About the Author

Bonnie Urquhart Gruenberg is a multifaceted person who wishes that sleep were optional. She is the author of the award-winning book *The Wild Horse Dilemma: Conflicts and Controversies of the Atlantic Coast Herds.* Horses have been her passion from infancy. For nearly two decades, she has spent countless hours researching and photographing the private lives of wild horses in both Western and Eastern habitats. She has been riding, training, teaching, and learning since her early teens, from rehabilitating hard-luck horses to wrangling trail rides in Vermont and Connecticut.

By profession, she is a Certified Nurse-Midwife and Women's Health Nurse Practitioner who welcomes babies into the world at a freestanding birth center in Lancaster County, Pa. She obtained her MSN from the University of Pennsylvania after completing her BSN at Southern Vermont College, and she spent 10 years attending births in tertiary-care hospitals before returning to out-of-hospital practice. Prior to her career in obstetrics, she worked as an urban paramedic in Connecticut.

She is the author of the award-winning textbook *Birth Emergency Skills Training* (Birth Guru/Birth Muse, 2008); *Essentials of Prehospital Maternity Care* (Prentice Hall, 2005); and *Hoofprints in the Sand: Wild Horses of the Atlantic Coast* (as Bonnie S. Urquhart; Eclipse, 2002), as well as articles in publications as dissimilar as *Equus* and the *American Journal of Nursing.* She is an artist and photographer and has illustrated all her own books.

In her vanishing spare time, she explores the hills and hollows of Lancaster County astride her horses Andante and Sonata. More information can be found at her Web site, www.BonnieGruenberg.com, and a collection of her photographs and artwork at BonnieGPhoto. com. Additional information about the Atlantic Coast horse herds is on the Web at www.WildHorseIslands.com.

If you liked this book, you may enjoy other titles by the author:

The Wild Horse Dilemma: Conflicts and Controversies of the Atlantic Coast Herds (Quagga Press, 2015)
The Hoofprints Guide Series (Quagga Press, 2015)
    Assateague
    Chincoteague
    Corolla
    Ocracoke
    Shackleford Banks
    Cumberland Island

Forthcoming
    Wild Horse Vacations: Where To See the East Coast Herds and What Else To Do While You're Visiting (Quagga Press, 2015)
    Wild Horses! A Kids' Guide to the East Coast Herds (Quagga Press, 2015)

Visit QuaggaPress.com for details.

Made in United States
North Haven, CT
16 June 2022

20327237R00083